THE LAST RESORT

THE LAST RESORT

A RETIREMENT VISION
FOR CANADIANS
AND HOW TO ACHIEVE IT

STEVE BAREHAM

HarperBusiness
HarperCollins*PublishersLtd*

http://www.harpercollins.com/canada

First edition

Canadian Cataloguing in Publication Data

Bareham, Steve
      The last resort : a retirement vision for Canadians and how to achieve it

A HarperBusiness book.
ISBN 0-00-638536-2

1. Finance, Personal - Canada. 2. Saving and investment - Canada. 3. Retirement - Canada - Planning. 4. Financial security. I Title.

HG179.B37 1997   332.024′01   C97-930256-0

97 98 99 ❖ HC 10 9 8 7 6 5 4 3 2 1

Printed and bound in the United States

Contents

THE LAST RESORT

Introduction

TRADITIONAL SOURCES OF RETIREMENT INCOME

For most Canadians, there are five immediately identifiable "potential" sources of retirement income:

- Canada Pension Plan (CPP);
- Old Age Security (OAS) and Guaranteed Income Supplement (GIS)—both to be amalgamated into a program called the Seniors' Benefit by the year 2001;
- Employment pensions;
- Registered Retirement Savings Plans (RRSPs); and
- Investments outside RRSPs.

Unfortunately, not every retiree can depend on income from all of these sources. In fact, someone who has never worked or saved may qualify only for the OAS and GIS, or their new incarnation, the Seniors' Benefit.

To more fully understand the retirement portfolio that is *potentially* available to Canadians, let's examine details of each of these sources of income.

The OAS, GIS, and Seniors' Benefit

The OAS is available to all Canadians over the age of 65, and it currently pays about $400 per month, per person. There are tax clawbacks for individuals and couples whose incomes exceed levels established by the federal government; single seniors earning more than $52,000 a year and couples with combined incomes of more than $78,000 receive no OAS benefits.

Also, the GIS is available only to retirees who have very low incomes—usually those receiving the GIS are living at, or below, the poverty line. Because the GIS and some provincial supplemental income programs are based on means tests and the amounts paid vary between provinces, the calculations can be complex. For the purposes of this book we'll assume the maximum amount available from Ottawa at the 1996 rate of $308 per person over the age of 65. Thus, the maximum income for a couple qualifying only for the OAS and GIS would be a total of the OAS and GIS maximums, which is $1,416 a month or $16,992 a year.

The Seniors' Benefit will be phased in over the next five years. At the time of this book's publication it was not clear precisely what rules and regulations will apply from year to year. Readers who believe they will qualify for this plan should request current information from the appropriate federal departments. The future of these programs is uncertain, so they are not included in projections in this book.

This leaves four other sources of potential income. Each deserves examination.

The Canada Pension Plan

Traditionally, the Canada Pension Plan is the one source of retirement income available to all working Canadians who have made the required contributions. Now, however, even the CPP appears to be in jeopardy.

Studies by federal and provincial governments and independent organizations have stated that by the year 2015 the current method of financing the Canada Pension Plan will produce insufficient funds to pay the greatly increased number of baby-boomer retirees leaving the work force. In the past there have been about four working Canadians to support each retiree, whereas by about 2015 the ratio is projected to drop to only two working Canadians per retiree. Under the existing "pay as you go" system, where no CPP reserve fund exists, this would constitute an untenable burden for about 18 million working Canadians trying to support 9 million retirees. Still, a recent study by Royal Trust reveals that 73 percent of Canadians are counting on the CPP as part of their financial future.

Government committees looking into the plan have recommended that CPP contributions be doubled immediately to keep the plan viable. This would mean raising individual contributions from the current 5.6 percent of insurable earnings to about 12 percent. And, even if the plan is solvent 20 years from now, many observers speculate that there will likely be costly changes for those working Canadians who consider CPP one of the pillars of their own retirement plans.

The possibilities for changing the CPP range from grim to horrendous:

- reducing monthly payments to retirees (currently a maximum of about $727 per month)
- raising the age of eligibility from the current 65 years to somewhere between 67 and 70 years
- eliminating inflation indexing. Benefits would increase by a rate of "inflation **minus** 1%"—which works out to a 1% cut each year
- and most drastic of all, eliminating the CPP altogether, or clawing back CPP entitlements from people receiving "high" incomes from employee pension plans, RRSPs or non-RRSP investments. The politicians of the day would determine the definition

of "high." If this gloomy prediction comes to pass, those Canadians who acted responsibly in planning for their retirements and who achieved a certain level of fiscal security, will face the irony of being the very people denied CPP funds even though they paid into the plan their entire working lives.

If the CPP Survives

As of late 1996, the maximum CPP benefits per working person paid $727 per month, or $8,724 per year. Clearly, this sum would provide only the most basic existence. Even "topped up" by an OAS or Seniors' Benefit allotment, readers must ask themselves two questions *now*:

1. Can you—and do you want to—depend on the CPP and the additional supplements as your sole sources of retirement income?
2. If these plans are still in place, will they produce enough income to sustain the quality of life you envision for yourself in retirement?

Employment Pensions

About 40 percent of working Canadians contribute to, and will receive, employment pensions. For those who have these pensions, they are a source of fiscal comfort. Unfortunately, many people seem to believe these pensions, combined with government programs, will be adequate. Studies suggest otherwise.

The "best" pension plans will, in fact, provide decent incomes, but these plans are rare. Most promise to pay an annual amount equal to only about 50 percent of "the average of a person's best five earning years"—and this is after 25 to 30 years of service. In dollar terms, then, a person earning an average of $45,000 over the last five years of work can expect to receive about $22,500 a year on retirement. Although many plans are indexed to inflation, this means they just keep pace with inflation. The real purchasing power of the pension never improves.

So, using current numbers, let's see what a couple, both aged 65, can expect to receive in a year of retirement if:

- one person has a work pension such as the one described, paying $22,500;
- this person qualifies for the maximum $727 CPP monthly payment ($727 x 12 = $8,724); and
- both qualify for the OAS or the new Seniors' Benefit at the maximum for a couple ($400 x 2), or $800 per month. (In this case, and given their income level, the couple would not qualify for the Guaranteed Income Supplement [GIS]).

The numbers break down as follows:

1.	Work pension	$22,500
2.	CPP	$ 8,724
3.	OAS/SB	$ 9,600
	Total	$40,824

If we use the lowest combined federal and provincial tax rate of about 30 percent, and a personal deduction of about $6,500 each, only the prime income earner will pay taxes—about $6,458 in total. Thus, the couple would "net" about $34,366 per year, or about $2,864 per month.

Once people have worked out such a projection based on their own situations—and they should do so at least 20 years before they reach the age of retirement—the logical question arises: "Will $2,864 per month in today's dollars finance my desired retirement lifestyle for 20 to 25 years?"

If you can answer "yes," perhaps you need to do nothing more.

If, however, you answer "no," then logic dictates that you should develop a plan to improve your income situation. (See worksheet in Chapter 3 to calculate and project your living costs today and in the future.)

Registered Retirement Savings Plans

Fewer than one-half of those Canadians who are eligible to do so contribute to RRSPs. This is a disappointing participation rate, especially given the welcome tax deduction relief government legislation provides, and the very attractive income tax-sheltering provisions offered as the funds within the RRSP compound and grow. Thanks to a steady stream of publicity in recent years, more and more people now seem to appreciate the importance of contributing to RRSPs, but the fact remains that many millions of Canadians have yet to commit themselves to these plans for their futures.

Retirement Investments outside RRSPs

Even fewer Canadians have retirement investments outside RRSPs than have savings in such plans. According to a national investment brokerage firm, people with non-RRSP retirement savings now constitute less than 10 percent of Canada's population—this number is expected to hold fairly constant over the next 20 years.

MORE BAD NEWS

Research also reveals that most Canadians, even those building employment pension plans and RRSPs, will still not have enough in those plans to support themselves as they would like to live in their retirement years.

These already inadequate pensions will be stretched even further because people are living longer. Life expectancies for both men and women are increasing steadily and dramatically. Many people will need their retirement nest eggs for their living expenses, travel, recreation, health care, for many years after they retire—particularly those who wish to retire early.

For example, Statistics Canada, in its 1991 publication *Population Ageing and the Elderly*, announces that by the year 2011 life expectancy for men "from birth" will increase to 77.2 years, and to 84.0 years for women. This compares with 73.0 years for men and 79.8 for women in 1986 (Catalogue 91-533E, page 10). Complicating the situation is the fact that people who actually live to age 65 tend, on average, to live even longer than these projections "from birth." On page 29 of the same publication Statistics Canada predicts that, on average, a woman who lived to age 65 in 1986 can expect to live about 19 years beyond that, to the age of 84. Similarly, a man who lives to age 65 can expect to survive an additional 15 years, on average, to the age of 80. Given continuing medical advances, baby boomers who begin to retire about the year 2011 may demonstrate even higher life expectancies.

So the retirement years now represent a very long period of time. We all want to live, but over this longer period of time inflation will steadily erode the real values of our pension funds. Even at a modest 2.5-percent inflation rate, we will face greatly reduced pension incomes over 30 years. For example, someone with a monthly retirement income of $2,000 today will need $4,092 to maintain the same lifestyle in 30 years. We will find it increasingly important that we not run down our retirement funds too quickly. We have to pay close attention to making the plan compound for as long as possible, particularly in the early years.

Demographers predict that there will be nearly 100 million North Americans over the age of 55 in the year 2011—one in four people (about 9 million Canadians and 90 million Americans). These 100 million older people will place incredible pressure on health care, retirement housing, and holiday resorts. In a society based on supply and demand, retirees with inadequate retirement plans may find themselves competing with one another as the "retired poor."

NOW FOR SOME GOOD NEWS

Despite such grim facts, retiring comfortably is within the grasp of most people. Commonsense solutions are available to those who take serious responsibility for determining their own future. This book provides these solutions. It speaks specifically to the millions of Canadians who want to know what they can do **now** to ensure they have enough money to permit them happy and active retirements—free of financial worries.

The Last Resort lays out clear, uncomplicated plans to show you how to arrange your finances. One of the most novel concepts in the book, in Chapter 9, explores retirement villages. Through this strategy you can bolster your financial health considerably by achieving two goals that may seem impossible and contradictory at first glance:

1. You would inject a considerable amount of money into your "spendable assets" to augment your retirement funds.
2. You would continue to live in "self-owned" luxury accommodation.

The Last Resort demonstrates many other financial and lifestyle planning concepts as well. Here are chapter highlights:

- Chapter 2 discusses where society is going and why knowing this information is so important to you.

- Chapter 3 discusses how to secure an adequate flow of income by building a no-risk strip-bond ladder—an original idea. A year-by-year plan spells out your annual goals and makes your retirement prospects more "doable." Discover how a couple about 45 years of age can guarantee themselves an $80,000 annual income at age 65 and for 14 years—$1,120,000 altogether—by investing $134,000 of RRSP funds today.

- Chapter 4 examines business people and entrepreneurs. They often have different ideas about retirement planning. Many have strengths that enable them to take unique, and equally successful, paths to fiscal security. Self-employment often translates into lower taxable incomes and, thus, reduced allowable RRSP contributions. Here are insights for people who choose to plot their own financial courses according to the realities of entrepreneurship.

- Chapter 5 looks at strategic life and investment planning (SLIP). This workable plan shows you how to determine where you are now, where you want to go and how best to get there. We all want to enjoy life, but our enjoyment is usually sporadic— it happens without planning. Here are some creative, simple strategies to make the things you really enjoy doing a routine part of your daily, weekly, and yearly life.

- Chapters 3 and 6 present "Navigating the Income Stream: A Doable, Low-Risk Plan" and "RRSPs: A Unique Short Course" respectively. These step-by-step formulas help you determine how much money you'll need to retire comfortably and precisely what you need to do to get it together. Detailed examples cover a wide range of income levels—even minimum-wage earners can prosper within RRSPs with only minimal sacrifices. Included are:

  - young people with no RRSP savings
  - minimum-wage earners who may be able to save only $50 per month

- parents in their thirties earning average incomes and saving only one-half of their RRSP allotments
- 40-year-olds with small savings, and
- mid-lifers with some RRSPs and savings that they consider inadequate.

(Readers will also find easy-to-fill-in "blank" worksheets throughout the book to prepare their personal plans.)

- Chapter 7 offers "Stock Approaches For an Edge (SAFE)," a commonsense approach to picking stocks according to a structured system for determining long-term economic and market directions. The chapter lists specific stocks and trends likely to be hot in the coming years.

- Chapter 8 probes how to mine the silver lining of your own real estate by "cashing out" your principal residence in favor of a smaller, luxury retirement cottage. Such a plan can inject tens, or even hundreds, of thousands of dollars into your retirement reserve. You want to do this *before* the bulge of baby boomers starts dumping their large homes for smaller and less expensive retirement accommodation in more rural areas.

- Chapter 9 details a step-by-step approach to planning and building a luxury retirement village where people of similar age and like minds live—a great comfort in retirement (see "The Retirement Village Concept" on the next page).

- Chapter 10 explores ways you can earn extra money and identify entrepreneurial ideas today for improving your own income flow tomorrow. Almost everyone is passionate about something that can also generate income for them. If you have interests, skills, or knowledge that give you great pleasure, why not plan to make money from them in your retirement and take advantage of the host of tax write-offs at the same time—travel, vehicle, home office—that come from self-employment?

- Chapter 11 summarizes more than two dozen money-making and lifestyle improvement lessons covered in the book.

THE RETIREMENT VILLAGE CONCEPT

Retirement villages are a commonsense housing and financial planning alternative for people at, or near, retirement age. These villages offer important benefits:

- secure tenure: self-owned affordable luxury housing
- money freed up for travel and recreational pursuits
- low or no maintenance worries
- privacy and quiet in your own home
- intelligent designs (one-story, wheelchair access)
- transportation access
- on-site assistance and health care for those who need it
- recreational offerings (tours, sports, theater, games, etc.)
- private garden plots
- meals on wheels for those who wish them
- bulk-buying potential to save more money
- socializing with others of like age and mind
- security and safety
- no worry about your home when you are on holidays
- manageability of a smaller house and lot.

Having your own retirement cottage also gives you another extremely important benefit—independence and control of your own destiny even in advanced age—a time when many people are ushered into retirement homes where they gradually lose the power to make their own decisions and become increasingly dependent on institutions where their quality of care varies widely.

*   *   *

The Last Resort promises you an optimistic look at retirement planning. Significantly, it demonstrates precisely how you can achieve peace of mind and quality of life today by creating a clear and doable retirement plan for tomorrow. You can, and should, have both.

Steve Bareham
April 1997

CHAPTER 1

The Visit

I pressed my forehead against the scratched Plexiglas oval and felt a dull ache spread through the window of the Dash 8 across the bridge of my nose from the subzero cold outside. The twin-prop droned noisily eastward, en route to Nelson, British Columbia.

Below stretched endless miles of wilderness. Rocky peaks jutted skyward from valleys fanning out like rivers, the vast jagged sea of the Valhalla Mountains, millions of square miles of summits, cliffs, forests, and countless lakes and streams. The ocean of craggy giants was unmarked by civilization—no towns, no roads. The mountains stood as they had at the dawn of creation.

Our shadow brushed over a rockslide that had carried away enough mountainside to fill a hundred football stadiums. In the avalanche's wake lay thousands of evergreen trees crushed and interlocked into an impenetrable mass of gargantuan pick-up-sticks.

I reached back in my mind to a high school geology course and snatches of facts about how such ancient mountains were formed. My long-term memory of the 30-year-old information was quickly exhausted. My mind moved to things less rigorous, the present and the reason for this trip—a reacquaintance with old friends I hadn't seen for years. The visit was an escape of sorts, but I really didn't know what I was escaping to. What was I going to do for a week with two "seniors" in their new retirement home?

I had tried to weasel out of the trip. My wife, Lorraine, had easily outmaneuvered me. She suggested several times that I'd be happier taking a short holiday rather than rambling around an empty house while she was away on a professional development course. I was touched by her selflessness until I overheard her say something to a friend about having saved her new copper-bottomed pots from being burned beyond redemption.

Then came the surprise telephone call from Gordon and Sara Strong, who insisted I get out of the city and spend some time with them.

Gordon really turned the screws after I blurted out how much I envied their recent retirement to lake country and lamented our own, dismal retirement prospects. Gordon expressed some incredulity at this. He said 20 years was plenty of time to prepare for retirement— "if you follow the proper courses of action."

I trotted out the old saw about how quickly the years were passing and how two decades seemed too short a time to get a good retirement plan in order.

He must have sensed the depth of my concern because he said I might benefit from learning how he and Sara had set up *their* retirement. "No" wasn't an acceptable option. The visit would be a "healthy tonic."

Yeah, right. I just hoped it wasn't more like a sleeping pill. I didn't need rest, I needed more time and more money.

I took some solace in learning that my flying companion shared some of my most pressing concerns. Her name was Carol. She was president of her own small Toronto software company. Confident and assertive, Carol was mightily chagrined about the weight Canada's tax system was exerting on her corporate shoulders. She was outraged that successive provincial and federal governments had, as she put it, routinely "misappropriated" billions of tax dollars collected annually from businesses and individuals. She reddened when alluding to the unconscionable level of government debt, to the fact that half of every tax dollar is needed to pay interest on those debts, and shook her fist to emphasize she was mad as hell at the prospect that the Canada Pension Plan was in jeopardy.

"Demographers told governments more than two decades ago that the CPP needed to be overhauled and that the pay-as-you-go approach wouldn't be enough to support the baby-boomer retirees. As usual, nothing was done. It was politically inexpedient to increase contribution levels. I suppose, if I had their pension plans, I wouldn't be overly concerned about CPP, either, but few of us common folk have gold-lined plans like that. You'd think some government some day would have the guts to tell it like it is, face reality and take some tough positions to get rid of the debt and the deficit. With half of our tax dollars freed up for something constructive, Canadians' lifestyle would improve dramatically over the long term."

Her view, I was certain, echoed those of many middle-class Canadians. I shared them myself.

Equally worrisome was a story I'd just read in the Toronto *Globe and Mail*. It predicted the popular retirement destinations for aging baby boomers over the next 30 years: Mexico, California, Arizona, Hawaii, and spots on the Mediterranean and other exotic locales in the sun for those with fat wallets. Plopping myself down in one of those places every January to March with a dozen good books was one of my most cherished retirement goals. The trouble was that I just couldn't convince myself that it would ever be possible given our finances.

Increasingly I found myself mired in a circular mental dialogue about the "what ifs" of financial planning. "What if we weren't putting enough away to secure our financial futures? What if the Canada Pension Plan isn't around when we retire? What if we make bad decisions with the RRSP funds we're accumulating?" These "what ifs" were driving me batty. I wished I could ask more optimistic questions, such as: "What if we had all the money we wanted? How would that change what we're doing now and what we plan to do in the future?"

Words by Somerset Maugham, the distinguished and wealthy author, answered my questions: "I found that money was like a sixth sense without which you could not make the most of the other five." That summed it up nicely. Money doesn't buy happiness or health, but a heavy purse does help make for a light heart.

Minutes later the plane taxied to a halt outside a small terminal. Carol and I said goodbye to each other and I grabbed my suitbag from the overhead rack. Bright August sunlight washed over me as I walked through the departure door.

Despite the decade since I'd last seen them, I recognized Gordon and Sara immediately. They were waving to me furiously from the other side of the waiting-area window. Gordon had been an engineer with an international construction company specializing in hydro-electric construction. Sara had tutored students in English in some of the non-English-speaking countries where Gordon's job frequently took them. This "gypsy" lifestyle was why we hadn't seen each other for so long. I was curious to see how they'd changed and what they were doing with their new-found leisure.

We embraced warmly. Gordon slapped me on the back and said, "Let's grab your bag and head for the lake."

In the parking lot I was ushered to a shiny new dark green Jeep YJ. Sara opened the passenger door and stepped up lightly into the back seat saying I'd enjoy the ride more up front. It wasn't the four-door sedan I had expected.

Gordon and Sara didn't look a day older. They were trim, tanned, and fit. Their conversation was quick, energetic, and good-natured.

"So, what do you think you'd like to do while you're here?" asked Gordon.

"Oh, I don't know," I answered. "I'm happy to just visit with you guys and maybe wring my hands a bit while I pick your brains."

"Well, I think we can come up with something a little more fun and productive than that," said Gordon. He turned to smile at Sara in the back.

"Sure, there's lots to do at the resort," said Sara. "I don't think you'll be bored. We'll make sure you get what you came for."

"What resort?" I asked.

"The Last Resort," said Gordon.

"What last resort?" I said, struck by the phrase.

Gordon and Sara laughed heartily.

"*Our* last resort," said Sara. "You'll see."

I didn't see but I smiled and pretended I did.

DAY 1

We drove through the small mountainside city of Nelson, B.C., heading onto the north shore of Kootenay Lake's west arm.

About four miles out Gordon turned into an opening cut into a row of dense old-growth cedar trees. A narrow dirt lane curved gently through greenery and down toward the water. About 100 yards farther along I saw a collection of cozy-looking cottages built among and beneath the trees. Each was surrounded by a well-maintained lawn and most sported colorful flowering foliage draped over archways and trellises, and ground flowers blossoming against the foundations. "Nice," I thought. "Houses that look like they belong."

We passed a wooden sign at the side of the lane that said "The Last Resort." "Okay," I told Sara, "now I get it."

Gordon pulled into the driveway of one of the cottages nearest the lake. "Here we are, home sweet home."

I looked around as we piled out of the Jeep. What an orderly place, cool, a pleasant moist aroma and green. Birds chirped in the trees overhead—peaceful.

Without thinking I said, "You said you lived in a retirement community. This isn't what I expected."

"I'm not sure what you expected," said Sara. "but we're proud of what we've built here. We think it's pretty special."

"It looks it. Who built this place?"

"We'll tell you all about it later. It's quite a novel approach,"

17

said Gordon. "There aren't many like it yet. You're going to see a lot more of them once you baby boomers start to retire and have to face the question of retirement housing."

"Yeah, retirement," I said. "Just a few years ago I never thought about it at all. Now it's got half the people Lorraine and I know worried sick that we're not planning adequately and that we're all going to end up paupers. If it weren't for the money, or lack of money, and the fact that retirement means getting older, it sure would be good to be able to quit work and just relax."

ENJOYING "DETIREMENT"

"We'll talk about that, too," said Sara, opening the front door. A thick, smoke-gray Oriental throw rug spread softly over the natural flagstones of the foyer. Even from the doorway I could see a profusion of plants, paintings, and other artwork.

"We've had lots of time this past year to think about life and living since we detired," Sara went on. "We've come to some interesting realizations. I know when you're young and busy with a career and a family, retirement looks like an appealing escape from it all. Once you do actually detire, though, you quickly come to appreciate the grim irony of this goal. We've done a 180-degree turn in coming to the view that detiring isn't about stopping—it's about starting."

"Did I hear you say *detired*?" I had to ask.

"Yes!" She laughed. "We call it detired. You're a writer. You know that 're' often means to go backward or withdraw, like reverse or retreat. Well, the prefix 'de' makes a word mean the opposite, as in activate and *de*activate. We find ending our nine-to-five existence quite the opposite of withdrawing. We're detired. We see this part of our life more as sowing, not reaping."

They laughed together again. They did that a lot. I gave that knowing smile that people give when they have nothing particularly intelligent to contribute. At the moment, in any case, I was more interested in the house.

"Great place," I said.

Gordon and Sara had designed it themselves, they said, as had each of the 20 owners of homes in the village. The only stipulations, I later learned, were that each house—or cottage, as the villagers called them—had to be single-story, with no more than 1,000 square feet of floor space, of timber or log construction, with cedar-shake roofs and cedar siding. These few rules gave the resort a pleasing uniformity of natural textures while allowing the owners considerable latitude in choosing exterior designs that suited their individual tastes.

The Strong cottage was log post-and-beam and appeared much larger than it was. Airy vaulted ceilings soared over an open-concept floor plan that joined the kitchen, living, and dining rooms. Walls gave privacy to the bathroom and two bedrooms only.

My room was very comfortable, again with vaulted ceiling, rustic log beams and vertical supports. A space-saving Murphy Bed was pulled down, already made, out of one wall. How many of those do you actually see in life? A roll-top desk and other furnishings suggested that the room functioned as an office when there were no guests. Clever space design.

Leaving me to unpack, the Strongs said we'd go down to the lake once I was settled in. While arranging clothes in the closet I noticed a burl plaque on the wall with carved letters. It read:

> Where are we now? At the most important spot in time you'll ever know—where history ends and the future begins. The past pales in fading memory and consumes needed energy. The future consumes yet more energy in wistful anticipation. Now—the present—is the only thing on which you can really count.
>
> —Anon

"Sounds like something from the sixties," I thought, "or the comment of an astronomer friend who likes to have a few glasses

19

of wine and then tries to convince listeners that time is flexible and, depending on where you were on the continuum, it moves neither forward nor backward."

Well, as far as I knew, time has a definite preference. People get older, not younger; you remember the past, not the future, and things decay from organized states into mushy lumps. Cosmologists might think they're onto something, but the theories didn't seem to have any effect on the finite lifespans of people here on earth.

Still unpacking, I made my way to the ensuite bath. It, too, was rustically decorated in keeping with the rest of the house: flagstone floor warmed by infloor radiant pipes, interesting driftwood art and numerous plants. And . . . another of those burl plaques. This time the message read:

> Man's greatest blunder has been in trying to make peace with gods instead of with neighbors.
> And his only enemy is himself and this due to his ignorance of this world and his superstitious belief in another.
>
> —Elbert Hubbard

So, Gordon and Sara were atheists and closet philosophers. Were these just decorations or were their guests expected to participate?

I followed Gordon as he led the way down a cobblestone pathway to a large floating dock at water's edge. Several boats were moored there. He beckoned me to a black aluminum craft with a large winch on the bow. I'd never seen anything quite like it. Low-slung and rugged-looking, it didn't resemble the shiny fiberglass jobs that usually fill marinas.

"It's a Duckworth jetboat," said Gordon, noticing my scrutiny. "Great for beachcombing. Hop aboard *The Ugly Duckling*."

With the top unzipped and lowered, Gordon turned on the

ignition. The engine rumbled, sparked, and settled into a burbling beefy purr as the underwater exhaust churned water at the stern. Sounds powerful, I thought, surprised to hear a V8.

We backed out of the dock and Gordon powered eastward into the arm. I settled back to take in the surroundings. Beautiful day, warm sunshine sparkling on the water, a few puffy cumulus clouds, and rounded mountains clad in emerald green. Not bad.

Within a half hour we'd cruised at speed out of the arm and across Kootenay Lake. Gordon steered into a sheltered and shallow harbor called Pilot Bay and snapped a rope to the eye of a floating buoy. Sara opened a cooler and passed around glasses filled with something effervescent.

"We'll have some champagne when we get back to shore, but for now this will have to do. Welcome to the Last Resort!" they said and we all clinked glasses.

I took my cue after the toast.

"I've got to say: the Jeep, the cottage, the boat. This does feel like a resort."

"You bet," said Gordon with a smile. "People never really grow up, only our playthings change. Most of us spend our working lives trying to make as much money as possible to raise our families, and later to buy houses, land, and all sorts of pursuits for pleasure. Well, nothing has changed for us in detirement. We still like many of these things, especially the pleasures, even more now that we have time to use and enjoy them. You'd better believe we plan to amuse ourselves doing whatever we want for as long as we can."

TAX-DEDUCTIBLE TOYS

"Well, I'm impressed," I said. "You must have done pretty well overseas to afford this lifestyle."

"It was okay," said Gordon, "but it wasn't working for a salary for 30 years that got us here."

"Lottery?" I asked.

"God, no!" said Gordon. "The trick is to use all your options and make some informed financial decisions. Take this boat."

"Okay," I said.

"Wise guy," said Gordon. "I mean this boat is one of our wise financial decisions."

"I always heard them described as holes in the water into which you pour money," I said.

"Yes, they are," he said laughing, "but this boat is half owned by our company, so half the cost and the expenses are tax-deductible. It takes some of the fiscal pain out of boat ownership."

"What kind of business are you running?" I had to ask.

"A furniture business," he replied.

"I think when Ottawa finds out about this I'll be visiting you in jail," I said.

"No way. It's all perfectly legal. We set up the business last year to make some extra money, have some fun while we're making it, and to maximize our tax write-offs. The business lets us do all these things and gets us out on the water at the same time."

"Your furniture must get awfully wet," I said.

"Very funny," he said. "Never mind, I'm sure you'll see the beauty of the plan. I think every retired couple should start some kind of business, especially ones that let you fulfill one of your key detirement objectives—to be able to spend money on things we enjoy and to pay as little tax as possible while we're enjoying them. We're going to do that until death, that kindly old nurse, finally puts us to sleep."

This made me shift a bit and Gordon noticed. He was smiling broadly. "Don't worry," he said, "we'll probably be around long enough to see you in detirement." Interesting, I thought, how any mention of death by older people makes you squirm. I could see, as 50 came into view, that I'd have to start making some attitude adjustments.

The afternoon passed quickly and our conversation touched on snippets of Gordon and Sara's "detirement" plan and philosophy.

They spoke about the headlong pursuit of baby boomers trying to achieve financial security for their retirements.

FROM BABY BOOMERS TO BABY GLOOMERS

"Your generation has had things pretty easy, historically speaking," said Gordon. "There were plenty of good career opportunities as the economy grew quickly in the sixties and anyone with half a brain did pretty well through the seventies and eighties, too. Despite this period of growth we're sensing that things are changing a bit in the nineties as the maturing baby boomers start to think about their own mortality at a time of government and corporate downsizing.

"You've gone from baby boomers to baby gloomers," he quipped.

"It's too bad," continued Sara. "All the publicity in recent years about excessive government debt and the unsure future of the Canada Pension Plan seems to be causing a real confidence crisis in your generation. We're only 20 years older, but given that we're already detired we have a better idea where we stand. We have to plan for only about 20 years of life whereas you need a crystal ball for about 40—maybe more if you're blessed with good genes."

"We have other friends your age," her husband chimed in, "and we find ourselves preaching that good mental and physical health are best secured by people who aren't overly anxious about either. Preoccupation's companion is stress, and stress is more damaging than most excesses humanity has invented. If we're seeing a preoccupation these days, it's among baby boomers who seem to think they're going to run out of money in retirement, have no pension plan, and lose government-sponsored health care just at the age when it becomes most important to them. Man, are we glad we're not in your shoes!"

We all had to laugh at his comment, but I had to point out that the gloomy scenario he painted wasn't necessarily impossible.

"No, it isn't," he agreed. "And giving you some peace of mind is one reason we wanted you to visit. Another reason is to share some good food and drink with us. And with that thought in mind, I think it's time we zipped home."

The food and wine were indeed good. An excellent Caesar salad, steak filets wrapped in bacon and smothered in Dijon gravy, and fresh stir-fried vegetables picked just before supper from the little garden behind the cottage. Gordon and Sara also took pride in serving a hearty bottle of burgundy that I learned they made themselves at a little cottage wine cooperative operating at the resort.

"Not bad for about $1 per bottle," said Gordon, "another of our little cost-saving strategies. We drink about two bottles of wine a week so it costs us about $8 per month. If we bought the wine at the liquor store, at an average cost of $8 per bottle, it would cost us $64 a month. As we see it, we're ahead $56 per month, or $672 a year. That little savings alone buys us airfare to the Baja."

Detiring after the meal to comfortable leather sofas in front of the fireplace, Sara poured brandies into warm snifters. We all sank back.

"Now," said Gordon. "Fill us in on why you're so anxious, as you described it on the phone."

So much for devil-may-care.

I'd mentally prepared for this moment but hated to break the mood with what seemed more and more like far-off worries that were perhaps a bit overblown. Still, he'd asked.

BABY GLOOMING

"Well," I said, "I guess the place to start is that pessimistic perspective of the future we talked about this afternoon. Given the state of government finances, I believe it's prudent not to rely on any form of government pensions by the time I hit 65. I could be wrong, and hope I am, but I'm sure that Canada Pension funds will end up going to people without work pensions or RRSPs. I doubt the Seniors' Benefit Program will survive past 2010 and, even if it does, only the poorest of the poor will qualify for it.

"The irony could be that those of us who saved our own money could see our access to the CPP either denied or clawed back, precisely because we took responsibility for ourselves and planned a decent level of retirement income.

"And people are living longer. As you mentioned, we have to somehow accumulate sufficient retirement funds to last for maybe 30 years after we retire. And once we're out of the workplace it's difficult to cope with either high inflation, which would drive prices up horrendously, or, conversely, low inflation which translates into miserly interest rates and lower returns on the interest-bearing types of investments retired people usually feel safest having."

"You could be right," said Gordon. "Knowing you have a plan to get you through even the worst-case scenario does offer a certain peace of mind. So, for the sake of conservative planning, it's smart to make your assumptions. If you're wrong and get CPP, or a piece of Seniors' Benefit funds, or if interest rates and inflation cooperate, it can only improve your situation, but I appreciate why you feel more comfortable looking at the worst case. Always overestimate expenditures and underestimate revenues—that's a good rule of thumb in any long-range financial planning."

"Right, it seems we can conjure up all kinds of possible future events that could throw a wrench in our planning," I went on. At times we feel things are pretty much out of our control and that nothing we can do will be good enough."

"Yes," said Gordon. "So what you need to do is learn how to plan for the future without giving up your enjoyment of life today. The trick is to approach the whole subject systematically and then follow the right steps."

DECIDING ON THE RIGHT STEPS

Preferring to take right steps rather than wrong ones I said, "Good. What right steps?"

"Well, before you plan how to get somewhere, you have to know where it is you want to go."

"Huh?"

He laughed. "Many people pursue the whole retirement planning process from the wrong end, by simply trying to accumulate funds without knowing what they're really likely to need. A common approach is to sock away as much money as possible. We have friends who are extremely well positioned financially, but they don't know how well off they are because they don't have a realistic perspective on their own future needs. It reminds me of a Kahlil Gibran proverb: 'Is not dread of thirst when your well is full the thirst that is truly unquenchable?'"

"I'm starting to think you guys spent the last 10 years at an ashram with some holy men," I said. "Maybe we'd all be happier if we gave away all our belongings and spent the rest of our days staring at the walls of some cave."

"You can if you want," said Gordon. "We plan to take off for the Baja in January to do some kayaking."

Sara laughed. "The point my husband the wit is trying to make is that if you don't have a fairly concrete handle on your long-term needs and goals, the whole process gets impossibly daunting. Everyone needs realistic markers to signify progress, and when you don't know exactly what you need it's difficult to keep focused. And a lack of focus can lead to a state of depression even though you might actually be doing quite well.

"We're seeing too many people your age forgoing life's pleasures now because they feel they can't afford to spend resources that need to be 'compounding.' I know compound interest is the big buzzword with financial planners these days, and it really is a remarkable thing. Still, it can become a bit of a drag when you start viewing every $1,000 today as $5,000, if only you tuck it away for 20 years."

"I know the feeling," I said, "but not tucking those thousands away might end up being a really bad move if we gloomers find out in 30 years that our worst-case scenarios were right."

"Oh, boy," said Sara, "it looks like we've really got our work cut out for us this week, Gord."

"Sorry, you guys," I said. "I'll try to keep my views a little less apocalyptic. Frankly, it would be nice to have a rosier perspective on this whole thing. So, how do I set some reasonable goals that will give us some peace of mind now and in the future?"

Beginning the Analysis

Looking at his watch, Gordon said, "Well, it's now after 11. How about we get to that tomorrow? It's been a long day and there's some information we'd like you to consider before we start on too many specifics. I would like to leave you with one thought tonight, though. Sam Goldwyn once said, 'For your information I'm going to ask you a few questions.' One question is, how much money do you think you need to adequately fund your retirement?"

"As a matter of fact I've thought about that a lot. I don't agree with the common wisdom that you need only 75 percent of the money you make in your last years of work. I guess that figure would suffice if you planned to live in retirement the way you did when you were working. But we want to get out of the country for the worst months of winter, and that's going to cost big money.

"So, we figure that in today's dollars we need to net at least $3,000 a month to live at home in Canada. Then, if we want to take off for a winter holiday for three months every year from January to March, and have to rent accommodation along with zillions of other baby boomers, we think that monthly figure should probably be tripled. That means we'll need $27,000 for nine months in Canada and $27,000 for the other three when we're on holidays—that's $54,000 take home or somewhere around $80,000 gross between the two of us."

I paused for effect.

"To gross $80,000 a year, assuming savings and GIC interest rates stay in the 5- to 6-percent range, we think we'd better have about $1.5 million saved by the time we retire!"

"Wow!" said Sara. "Big numbers. It seems every time I talk to younger people, million-dollar-plus figures pop up. Depending on age, of course, and how much a person has managed to save, the numbers can be accurate. Just as often, though, they're too high. Our job this week is to determine if these numbers are accurate, or excessive, for *your* situation."

"In that vein, how do your pension funds look now and what kind of equity do you have in your house?" Gordon asked.

"Well, that's the bad news," I said. "I have no work pension and both of our RRSPs together total only about $134,000. And Lorraine's work pension won't produce much on her retirement. We have no investments outside our self-directed RRSPs. We could walk with a whack of cash if we sold the house, but then we wouldn't have a place to live, so that seems like a bad idea.

"So, even making our maximum contributions to our RRSPs and getting a consistent 10-percent gain every year won't get us anywhere near to the $1.5 million by the time I'm 65," I said. I felt good that I'd strung all the figures together coherently, even if I didn't like the way they added up.

Something to Sleep On

Gordon had been poking at his calculator as I spoke.

"No, it won't," he said after a minute. "But what if I told you your current RRSPs alone could bring you $80,000 a year with no risk for the years 2017 to 2029, and that the equity in your house in 20 years, plus all the remaining years of pension contributions, will get you well over your $80,000-a-year goal? Congratulations, my friend, you're a pretty rich man!"

"Hey, I think you'd better get your calculator checked. I've gone over the numbers many times and I don't get such a pretty picture."

Gordon looked unfazed. "Fair enough, I'll let you check my

calculations yourself, but I can prove your existing $134,000 in RRSPs is worth more than $1 million. Your situation is better than you know. I was going to save this for later, but maybe now's a good time to try to get your mind shifting from the need to accumulate a huge sum of money in only 20 years to a perspective that spreads your time frame and the power of compounding over a much longer time span—specifically, your whole life.

"Look at this sheet that details how relatively small investments in quality government strip bonds today can secure income for you for quite a few years in the future. It's too bad so many people just look at the million-dollar figure and get pessimistic about the long line of zeroes. It's just as productive, and more doable, for you to look at your retirement from the perspective of what you need on a year-to-year basis.

"I'm not saying strips are the way to go, but for risk-averse people they're one of the safest strategies and they're dead easy to understand. You could well earn considerably higher rates of return in equities, except with equities you have risk. With strips we can paint an accurate picture. We can nail down precise costs and, more important, precise returns for each retirement year. If you can get higher returns some other way, so much the better, but strips make for an easy-to-understand planning model."

I took the sheet of paper he held toward me. It read:

STRIP BOND COSTS AND MATURITY VALUES

Maturity Date	Investment Today	Yield (%)	Maturity Value
2011	$ 6,289	8.68	$ 20,000
2012	5,703	8.78	20,000
2013	5,162	8.89	20,000
2014	4,695	8.95	20,000
2015	4,338	8.95	20,000
2016	3,967	8.94	20,000
2017	3,797	8.68	20,000
2018	3,557	8.58	20,000
2019	3,243	8.66	20,000
2020	2,914	8.89	20,000
2021	2,846	8.39	20,000
2022	2,634	8.45	20,000
2023	2,400	8.52	20,000
2024	2,018	8.90	20,000
2025	1,865	8.87	20,000
2026	1,729	8.84	20,000
2027	1,702	8.56	20,000
2028	1,597	8.49	20,000
2029	1,571	8.43	20,000
2030	1,550	8.50	20,000
TOTAL	**$63,577**		**$400,000**

(Note: This table is provided for demonstration purposes only. While face values and interest yields were current at the time of writing, current purchase prices and yields change. Interested readers can obtain these from the appropriate institutions or financial advisers. For a complete description of strip bonds see Chapter 3.)

When I looked up after scanning the figures for a few minutes Gordon added, "You can see that what you need to get your $80,000 in 2017 is $15,188—four times $3,797. And, if you extend out 14 years to 2030, you can see you need to invest only $6,200 now to get another $80,000 that year. This means that, to secure $80,000 a year for 14 years, from the time you're 65 until you're 78, requires only $133,692 (4 x $33,423), not an insignificant sum, but also one that a lot of people who have been serious about their RRSPs for 10 to 15 years may already have—you and Lorraine, for example. By approaching your retirement years as an extension of your pre-retirement investment years, you can see that even a person 45 years of age today can benefit from 30-plus years of compounding interest.

"I'm not saying your retirement savings task is complete, but you still have 20 years to save, plus some other strategies we're going to cover in the coming days."

My mind was busy calculating. It quickly became clear we *did* have enough for quite a few years at decent income levels. Fourteen strip bonds each worth $20,000 a year beginning in the year 2017, and ending in 2030, would have face values of only $33,423 today. Multiply that by 4 and the cost today would be $133,692 to guarantee $80,000 a year for 14 years. Multiply the 14 years by $80,000 a year and you get—$1,120,000! Gordon was right.

He sensed my change of mood.

"But we'll get into all this more in the next day or two. Tonight, try to go to bed viewing it my way. It's time you wore rose-colored glasses for a change."

We bid each other good-night. I lay on the Murphy bed listening to the wash of waves on the shore as I drifted into sleep. I wondered exactly what Gordon and Sara had in mind. It seemed my well *was* fuller than I thought.

31

"I skate to where I think the puck will be."

—Wayne Gretzky

CHAPTER 2

Divining the Future

Chapter Goal: **What you don't know about the future can hurt you. Demographics and trends promise to affect all our lives profoundly in the coming years.**

DAY 2, Morning

I awoke to lemon-tinged sunlight filtering through slits in horizontal oak blinds. A carpet of fog lay over the water. Out of the fog poked black-green mountains, floating on the mist. The world hovered quiet and surreal.

Just as I was about to turn away from the scene I noticed some movement near the water's edge. I could discern a human form half obscured by the early morning mist. The apparition flowed slowly from one strange pose to another, its extended arms moving gently up and down. The movements reminded me of a very large bird.

Curious, I thought, but this wasn't the time to dawdle.

I showered quickly and pulled on jeans and a sweater. The tantalizing aroma of coffee drew me to the kitchen. Gordon was sitting on the patio, cup in hand, gazing contentedly at the new day.

"Is it always like this?"

"No, not always," he said, raising his mug in greeting. "We get our share of cloud. The locals call it the Kootenay Greys. It

35

doesn't bother me. I'll take cloud any day over cold or wind, or both. I've lived in Saskatchewan, you know."

"I saw someone kung fu-fighting down by the lake a few minutes ago, or is the mist and light playing tricks?"

"No, that's Cosmo Northey."

"Cosmo?" I asked.

"Yeah, odd name. Real nice guy. Had a chain of martial arts studios. Still owns some but has managers now and spends most of his time here at the resort. He's a good friend. Has quite a bit of green, lives a pretty Spartan life. I think you'll enjoy meeting him."

We heard dishes clinking inside. Gordon motioned me in for a wonderful country-style breakfast of lake trout, pulled from the water the day before, poached eggs, and hash browns. While I might be concerned about my retirement fund's growth, clearly I needn't have the same concern for my waistline.

"So, what's up today?" I asked.

"Well, we thought we'd spend some time trying to divine the future," said Sara. "Later, when our brains are tired, we'll visit friends down the lake."

"Divining the future? Sounds like group therapy," I said. "I hope you guys don't mind me taking up your time with all this."

"Not at all," said Gordon. "We enjoy it. Figuring out where the world is going and how to best survive in it is fun. If it isn't fun it's stress, and we don't have time for that."

"Sounds good to me," I said. "So what have you got in mind to discuss?"

"Well, since you're here for a few days, we've come up with a curriculum of sorts. We'll blend it, of course, with a measure of fun and recreation. How about we start today with the environmental scanning of SIPing and SLIPing?" said Gordon.

"Somebody's got a drinking and walking problem?" I guessed.

Gordon chuckled. "SIP is an acronym for Strategic Investment Planning, and SLIP stands for Strategic Life and Investment Planning. They have nothing to do with the assumptions you leapt to.

Although, if you're a good boy and we get the results I expect from the process, I do have an old bottle of Cragganmore Highland Malt that I'll let you sample."

"I don't know where you learned your motivational skills, Gordon," I said deadpan, "but I'm insulted that you think I could be bribed with a drink of scotch."

Gordon looked at me quizzically.

"I could, however, be talked into this for *two* drinks."

Beneath our shared laughter I was thinking, "Strategic planning—Oh god."

Aloud I said merely, "I've done some reading about strategic planning and all I've seen it applied to is organizations."

"I know," said Sara. "We don't think anyone has applied it quite like this before. A friend took us through the process a while back. I was dubious at first, too. I'd read a bit about strategic planning overseas and, frankly, had chalked it up to another management buzz phrase that would go the way of the dodo and MBO—Management By Objectives.

"Cosmo," said Gordon.

Sara and I both looked at him.

"It was Cosmo who took us through strategic planning. He was down practicing by the water this morning. Remember, I told you we wanted you to meet him."

"Right," I said.

"Well," Sara continued, "after Cosmo did his shtick on us we were converts. We've seen strategic planning in action and we're both convinced it's a great tool not only for organizations, but also for people who want a system and structure to improve their life plans."

I was skeptical. "Okay, but be gentle."

Gordon laughed. "Don't worry. Think of yourself as Civil War General George Stedman."

"Huh?" I said.

"He was one of the first strategic planners," said Gordon.

"Cut off from his lines by enemy forces, he used strategic planning to scan his environment, analyze his strengths and weaknesses, and establish a plan."

"So, what did General George do?" I asked readily.

"I thought you'd never ask," said Gordon. "In the true spirit of strategic planning, he did a quick environmental scan and then assembled his troops and said: 'Men, I want you to fight vigorously and then run. And, since I'm lame, I'm going to start running now.'"

After breakfast Sara invited me back out to the patio to the comfort of a weathered, gray Adirondack chair. Gordon was arranging some papers on the table and looking professorial with a pair of half-frame glasses on his nose.

"There's a bit of future-watch information we'd like you to wrap your mind around before we start 'plugging in' your own thoughts about your personal future, goals, desirable actions, and all that. By morning's end we'll have scanned the future and, I hope, have generated some ideas about the types of decisions and actions you may want to consider. Tomorrow we'll tackle some planning specifics and, then, when you get home, you can repeat the process with your better half and make whatever adjustments you feel are necessary to make the plan work for both of you."

"Okeydokey," I said.

"Sara and I have been researching what we think will be some of the significant trends that'll affect us in the coming decades and that should therefore play a big part in our long-range planning today. What we want is your assessment of this future we predict and your analysis of how all this is likely to affect *your* finances and your life."

WHATEVER THE FUTURE WILL BE . . .

"The topics we've assembled aren't all-inclusive, but they do hit on some of the major areas. They are:

- the aging population, life expectancy, and health;
- the economy today and where it's likely to be in two decades;
- recreational interests;
- what the elderly are going to do with their time 25 years from now;
- holiday getaways;
- where the elderly will want to live and pass their time enjoyably;
- personal accommodation; and
- investment markets in the coming decades.

"So, how about you read this stuff and we'll discuss what you think of the trends we cover and our assumptions." With that he handed me a package of papers and I began to read.

OUR AGING POPULATION, LIFE EXPECTANCY, AND HEALTH

In 1995 the first of Canada's more than 9 million baby boomers turned 50. Many of them will begin early retirement in the year 2000. The number of retired people will increase dramatically over the next two decades. Statistics Canada reports that there will be about 5 million Canadians aged 65 years and older by the year 2011, almost 15 percent of the country's projected population of 33.4 million people at that time.

Although 65 is still the "magic" number for most retirees, many people will try to leave the workplace early, before they reach that age. Fully 27.4 percent of Canada's population in 2011 will be over the age of 55—more than 9 million Canadians. (I include people 55 years of age and older in this overview because this is the age at which most people begin to seriously contemplate retirement and change their saving and spending patterns.)

The effects this massive bulge of older people will have on

society and the economy are difficult to anticipate fully, but there can be no doubt they will be dramatic.

For the year 2011 Statistics Canada projects that the population of the country will be as follows:

Age Group	Percentage	Number of People
0–4	5.7	1,904,210
5–9	5.8	1,937,618
10–14	6.1	2,037,839
15–19	6.6	2,204,875
20–24	6.4	2,138,061
25–29	6.5	2,171,468
30–34	6.5	2,171,468
35–39	6.6	2,204,875
40–44	6.8	2,271,690
45–49	7.8	2,605,762
50–54	7.7	2,572,354
55–59	6.8	2,271,690
60–64	6.0	2,004,432
65–69	4.5	1,503,324
70+	10.2	3,407,534
TOTAL	**100**	**33,407,200**

Note: 9,186,980 people will be aged 55 or older in 2011.

One Hundred Million Strong

If we include the U.S., the situation becomes even more remarkable. With all North Americans 55 years of age and older in our calculations, the number of potential retirees jumps to about 100 million people in 2011, double the number in this age group today.

Most of these people are going to be healthy. Many of them will have some disposable income from work pensions, government pensions, and self-directed retirement plans. They are going to be active and demanding, and they'll have high expectations for themselves.

A Global Perspective on Aging

We're seeing a tremendous rise in the number of older people outside North America, too. In 1950, according to the United Nations, 128 million people over the age of 65 were alive. By the year 2025, the UN projects there will be 825 million people over this age. In the "developed nations" the same year, one in five people will be more than 65 years old—that's 66 million in Canada and the U.S. alone.

In the less developed countries, the ratio of people this age and older in 30 years' time will be only one in 12, but the much larger populations in less developed nations mean that a full 70 percent of the elderly people alive on the planet will live in those countries.

What constitutes "old"? As the boomers passed into their forties, that decade ceased to represent the "aging" landmark it once did. What will be "old" in 2000? Probably not even age fifty. Maybe, one day, "old" will simply be your age when you die.

Live Long and Prosper

Canadians are also living longer. This trend is expected to continue. Today, most men aged 65 can expect to live to about 80, and most women to 84. This contrasts with a life expectancy of only 48.2 years for men and 51 years for women in 1901, and 69.3 years for men and 76.3 years for women as recently as 1971.

People in their forties today, then, need to plan for at least 15 to 20 years of retirement after the age of 65 and maybe longer. Better health care and health-care research continue to improve our life expectancies, too.

How long you need to plan your own income flow becomes a very important part of your retirement strategy. Obviously, you can plan for the average age of mortality, or you can assume you're going to live longer and will need income to the age of, say, 100.

The numbers actually demonstrate that the chances of living to be "very old" are quite slim. According to Statistics Canada, only one in 20 people will live to 95 years of age. The bad news for men is that, of the "very old" population in the 95-year range, the ratio will be three women for every one man.

Alive but Disabled?

There is an important aside in this discussion about living longer. While life expectancy is lengthening quite quickly by historical standards, a difference between life expectancy and "disability-free" life expectancy remains.

According to Statistics Canada, the disability-free life expectancy is 9.4 years (74.4 years of age) for women aged 65 today, and only 8.1 years (73.1 years of age) for men. Be aware that the last years of your life may include health problems. Take this into account when planning various activities and travel in the years immediately following your retirement.

What Does All This Mean?

The elderly will be a very powerful force in the coming decades, particularly in North America. They will wield considerable clout in our economy, politics, social services, health-care services, the focus of scientific research, housing, recreational and other services. Where society's concentration in the 1950s and '60s was on children who needed schools, larger homes, clothing, and so on, these numbers point to a shift in focus to these same people in 2015 and the years following as they continue, at this later stage in life, to be a bulge in the population that can't and won't be ignored.

Retirees may demand state-of-the-art health-care facilities in smaller centers away from increasingly crowded, polluted, and crime-ridden cities. This would be in marked contrast to the current trend of locating the best hospitals in a few large cities across the country. It seems feasible that technology and demand could cause such a shift. Excellent health care that becomes transportable to smaller communities would remove one of the factors that has traditionally tied elderly people to large urban centers.

Geography

An important part of the retirement-planning process is thinking about where you want to live when you retire. For some people this question may seem easy: "Of course I want to be near my friends and family." This probably means staying put in a city since that's where most of Canada's population resides.

There are, however, some important societal changes and shifts that deserve your consideration—such as health care—before you can make a confident decision:

1. What is your "home" community going to be like in 2015? Is crime on the rise? Will this continue? Will the costs of living/taxes be higher there than elsewhere? Will this matter to you? What about transportation, busy streets, pollution?
2. If you own a home, can you pay for it fully by the time you retire? What amount of money is that asset likely to represent? Could it be converted into a new, perhaps smaller house in a less expensive real estate market to "free up" a large sum of cash? What impact could this have on your retirement finances?

Some sociologists predict an exodus from large urban centers early in the next millennium as people at and nearing retirement age seek safety, a better quality of life, cleaner places, peace and quiet. Many of these people may "cash out"—that is, sell their real estate in urban areas where prices have traditionally been highest.

Here's the rub. If many people wait until 2010 to sell, they could create such a glut of houses for sale in the large urban markets that prices overall could plummet. Conversely, prices

43

are likely to escalate dramatically in the most desirable regions of the country—the places with the best climate and scenery where retirees would most likely want to settle. The point is: don't get caught in the rush to unload houses. Those who believe this exodus will take place should act to divest themselves of their urban or suburban homes before the rush begins. Consider renting for a few years before you retire and investing the cash from the sale of your home. This may be a very good strategy for you to grow your retirement fund.

Following the same train of thought, property in smaller, perhaps more rural communities may become pricey quite quickly once the exodus begins. So, if you sell in the city, make sure you know where you want to go when you retire and consider buying a piece of property there and holding it until you're ready to retire.

> **Country and town: it should always be that way round. The country was there before the town. Country people can live without the town—not the other way around.**
>
> **—John Seymour**

The Economy

Currently the Canadian and U.S. economies look quite promising. They are experiencing:

- low inflation;
- low interest rates;
- tolerable rates of unemployment;
- increasingly efficient manufacturing sectors;
- a climate of high corporate earnings and profits—critical if equity markets are to do well;
- a commitment from the federal and provincial governments to reducing their deficits and debts;
- growth in world demand for Canadian and U.S. products and resources;

- more "high-level" jobs for younger people as baby boomers begin to retire;
- focused saving and investment attitudes among many North Americans as they near retirement; and
- more savings, which mean more money to invest. This bodes well for corporate capital and research and development.

In the latter part of the twentieth century, there seems to be reason for at least a decade of economic optimism. As long as inflation and interest rates remain low and the global economy doesn't turn down into recession, North America should prosper. This scenario should be heartening, particularly for the 40-plus segment of the population that needs several years of high returns in RRSPs and other investments.

However, a new dynamic may come into play between the years 2005 and 2010, when tens of millions of North Americans may drastically change their investment strategies and spending habits as they focus completely on "retirement mode."

This preoccupation will see mutual fund investments in this country grow from $137 billion in 1995 to an estimated $500 billion by the year 2002. By this period in life most people have made all their major purchases—house, vehicles, appliances—and they start socking away funds for that inevitable rainy day. People also become more discerning about their expenditures and begin to ask themselves, "Do we really need this?" As often as not, the answer will be "no."

Between the ages of 55 and 65 many people will also look at downsizing their real estate, living in smaller accommodation and, again, requiring fewer things in this reduced space and with their different priorities. Starting early in the next millennium, purchases of durable consumables could nosedive as this demand significantly shrinks.

Of course, this shift away from the traditional areas of

expenditure would translate into increased demand in other areas:

- Anything to do with recreation suitable for older people—golf will be hugely popular;
- All products and services in the travel industry— adventure tours down the Amazon or in little-traveled areas of Africa or the far north;
- Products designed to serve the needs of aging bodies (firmer mattresses, new types of shoes, revolution in the packaged goods industries);
- Home fitness as this older group opts for the comfort and privacy of their homes for exercise rather than public gyms;
- Health products: aging male boomers with prostate problems spell a windfall for medical advancements in this area, as do menopausal women for hormone replacement therapy research; and
- If you really want to look down the road—about 30 years—the funeral services business will be one of the biggest growth industries.

Despite these expanding areas, the bottom line is that retired people tend to be much more frugal than younger people. The North American economy could therefore feel the pinch as these 100 million people question every expenditure.

Doubtless the aging baby boomers will also prove very expensive for society. In 15 or 20 years they'll start making serious demands on our health-care and government-pension systems.

Discussions are currently taking place at the senior levels of government about the Canada Pension Plan and the much publicized concern that the smaller number of working Canadians will not be able to support the sudden onslaught of people expecting to claim their pensions. Mathematically, CPP contributions will have to double or triple to build up a reserve for the boomers to come.

Stocks

Recent years have seen baby boomers pouring money into stocks and equity mutual funds in the mad dash for retirement security. Fortunately, the markets and world economy have been quite cooperative.

Note, too, that the same demographic statistics that have seen money pouring into equities in recent years could also see money flooding out as the boomers near retirement and seek more conservative investments (bonds and other such interest-bearing instruments) to guarantee them reliable annual incomes. People at this stage in life dislike uncertainty and avoid risks in the stock market.

If this scenario plays out, a lot of people could lose interest in equities rather suddenly, starting early in the third millennium. You may not wish to have your retirement nest egg in equities while others withdraw billions of dollars from these investments. The economy won't necessarily worsen; people may simply change their preferences for where they invest their money with the least risk.

Bonds and Interest Rates

Whenever people are considering long-term investments, they must weigh the advantages and disadvantages of equities versus interest-bearing instruments. The concern with interest-bearing instruments such as strip bonds is that if higher inflation returns people will find themselves locked into rates of return that won't keep pace with rises in their cost of living. While it is true that the re-emergence of inflation would spell disaster for conservative bond investors, there is reason to believe this scenario is not likely to play out.

The reason is linked directly to the fact that the aging boomers are saving as never before. Hundreds of billions of dollars are going to find their way into equities, mortgage and bond mutual funds, guaranteed investment certificates, treasury bills, Canada Savings Bonds, and the like. With this amount of money flowing into the monetary marketplace over the next 20 years, it will be difficult to increase interest rates significantly. Consider also the interest-dampening effect of Canadian provincial and federal governments continuing their attack on their own deficits and debts. Again, this will mitigate against pushing up inflation.

Many economists agree with this forecast. John Kenneth Galbraith sums it up best in his recent book *A Journey Through Economic Time*: "With more savings available, the rate of interest would fall, and investment opportunities that were hitherto unprofitable would now become attractive."

Galbraith wasn't writing about strip bonds, but the basic economic premise holds true—simple supply and demand—a high level of savings means a surplus of money available for borrowing. A surplus of such funds translates into low interest rates because the price of capital equals the rate of interest.

Add into this mix the fact that an aging population doesn't want prices rising too rapidly and the stage is set for a long period of stable, low inflation and interest rates.

If these assumptions prove correct, the 8-percent-plus strip-bond rates of return could look very good about the year 2010 when millions of people will become nervous about holdings in equities and will go looking for good returns in fixed-income instruments. It can be scary to lock your money into long-term investments. All anyone can do is try to apply logic to what's going to happen and make the best decision at the time. This could mean spreading the risk and the return by putting, say, 30 percent of your retirement funds in strip bonds and the rest in other investments.

AN ANALYSIS OF THE FUTURE SCAN

It took me about half an hour to read and digest all that Gordon had written. Gordon and Sara had been re-reading it and making notes, too. We all finished about the same time.

"So," said Gordon, "what are your first thoughts?"

"I knew about the boomer demographics in general terms," I said, "but I must admit that when you see the actual numbers the concept is a lot more impressive."

"Well, we strive to impress," said Gordon, "but how do you see what you've read affecting *your* life?"

"Right. Well, I made some notes using your subheads. For example, on the rapidly aging population and where we decide to live, it's clear to me that things could get a little crowded in the places where we retirees gather. Conversely, it may also mean some great opportunities for anyone who manages to identify the so-far-undiscovered areas where retirees might like to live if they start feeling overcrowded where they are.

"I can certainly see cities such as Vancouver, Toronto, and Montreal as less pleasant places to live in 20 years. Although Vancouver's weather isn't as extreme as weather is in other major cities, all these cities are already crowded, it takes far too long to get around, and crime and pollution are getting worse every year. Give me a smaller center where I don't have to drive or ride a bus to get through my daily routine and where locking my door isn't a major priority, and I think retirement would be far nicer.

"In any case, I can see it makes sense to think about where we really want to retire.

"Lorraine and I always assumed we'd stay in the city, but maybe we should rethink that. Maybe we really could get a nicer place to live, plus have an extra $150,000 in our bank account after selling an expensive city home. Those are both pretty compelling considerations.

"I think something happens to a lot of boomers as they get older. The city lights just don't seem to hold the same appeal that they did when we were in our twenties and thirties when we were interested in more gala social events: concerts, plays, nightclubs, eating out. I know Lorraine and I feel real peace and relief when we get out of the city to someplace rural and quiet. This could be one of those later life tendencies that'll catch on in a big way and end up leaving the cities much less popular places to live.

"And your point is well taken about getting out of urban real estate before the rest of my generation thinks about it and we all put our houses on the market at the same time. To be a few years ahead of the retiring boomer pack, we might have to plan to sell in about five or six years, before the supply really exceeds the demand.

"I was also struck by the lengthening lifespans for men and women and how important it is to plan for three whole decades *after* retirement. It's kind of a drag because it means saving money today you may never get to spend. Yet it's necessary if you believe the numbers and don't want to be destitute in the last few years of your life.

"I appreciated the information about how long we're likely to be disability-free after retirement just as much. Living to 80 sounds like quite a while to me now, but if the averages are right and we can look forward to being disability-free until only our mid-seventies, we'd better not wait too long to travel and do the things we've always dreamed about, assuming we'll have lots of time in our late sixties. I don't see many 80-year-olds globe-trotting, so it would make more sense to plan larger expenditures for travel and recreation between the ages of 65 and 75 and then assume that you might want to, or have to, taper these expenses off.

"It also occurred to me that this growing number of older people seems to be viewed largely as a huge societal and economic negative—these millions of old people will threaten to bankrupt the nation. Too bad the retirement groups aren't mounting public relations campaigns to portray the aged as a valuable resource *now* instead of a liability. Maybe there's a job for someone like me in a few years."

Gordon and Sara seemed content to just listen, so I continued.

"The 100 million retirees are also going to make things a little crazy at holiday destinations, I suspect. Prices for accommodation, food, and the rest will probably skyrocket at traditional resort locations. Maybe this will mean the resorts in Hawaii, Arizona, and the like will be patronized only by the rich and that we average folk, with our average pension nest eggs, will be frozen out by the prices. Things are pretty expensive already, especially at the nice places where you don't have to worry so much about ailments like Montezuma's Revenge. Once there are 100 million of us scrambling for rooms and facilities, prices could really shoot up.

"Then there's the economy. I agree that all the money being pumped into pension plans and RRSPs makes for a pretty good investment climate in the coming decade or so—if, that is, inflation and interest rates stay low.

"It also struck me as plausible that I might not want to be anywhere near the stock market when the boomer retirement bulge really takes hold and people take their money out of equities to put it into safer interest-bearing instruments. The same movement that is driving the market up today can bring it down even faster if people start yanking billions out to put into bonds, GICs, and the like."

I felt I'd been talking too much. I know I'd repeated Gordon's points as I understood them.

"So, what do you guys think?" I ended feebly.

"We think you've hit on a lot of the important points," said Sara. "It's a good start to the environmental-scan part of SLIPing."

"I've always prided myself on being able to slip with the best of them," I admitted. "What's next?"

"Perhaps it's a good time to analyze where you are now so we have a better picture of the size of hill we have to climb," said Gordon.

There are people fate can never keep down. They stride confidently forward, taking the best that life affords. They do not scheme, nor trim their sails to catch the wind of popular opinion. They are ever alert to whatever crosses their path and when it comes, they appropriate it, and tarrying not, move steadily forward once again.

— adapted from Elbert Hubbard

CHAPTER 3

Navigating the Income Stream: A "Doable," Low-Risk Plan

Chapter Goal: To present a very low-risk plan to show how even a relatively small amount of money can produce a secure, sizable income for retirement.

DAY 2, Afternoon

"I want to get back to one of your comments from last night," I said. "It had something to do with me being a pretty rich man. I like the sound of that, but just saying it doesn't make me feel very rich."

"That's because you're looking at too short an investment horizon," said Gordon. "You have only 20 years to retirement, and even if you're very deliberate about pension contributions and other investments this isn't enough time for you, or for most people, to accumulate $1.5 million.

LOOKING LONG TERM

"My premise is that at age 45 you should be viewing your interest-compounding horizon as at least 40 years, assuming you live to 85. This isn't unlikely for at least one of you. In realizing your fiscal planning it's critical that you include:

1. the number of years *until* retirement, *plus*
2. the years *after* retirement, because your funds will continue to grow in an RRIF (Registered Retirement Investment Fund) for all the years following—perhaps 20 years or longer.

"Too many people think only about the years *until* retirement as saving and interest-earning years. This badly skews reality. It explains why so many people think a comfortable retirement is out of their reach.

"I can show you easily what I mean. I'll use the strip-bond model in my notes that you read last night. You may be able to earn higher returns in the stock market, or through equity mutual funds, but there are risks involved with equities and, for the sake of laying out a dependable, easy-to-understand plan, strips work nicely.

"If you choose the stock-market route, your retirement fund *could* grow more quickly with returns above the 8- to 9-percent range, but of course there's always the risk that your RRSP could also lose value if our markets were to hit a prolonged economic downturn.

"We like strip bonds because they're relaxed, feel-good interest instruments. They can make you wealthy slowly without extracting their pound of stress. Decades in advance you'll know what interest they're going to pay and precisely what your annual income flow will be. Their dependability makes them very attractive for retirement planning, and if you can secure your retirement with income levels where you want them to be without taking risks, why take any?

"A couple of observations before we begin," he said. "First, for the purpose of the scenario we're going to work up now, we'll use strip bonds with long maturity dates. They provide a simpler illustration of capital accumulation that anyone can understand. Be aware, however, that many financial advisers currently recommend going short term on bonds since they assume inflation is going to return. Then interest rates will rise, they say, and you'll be able to lock into better yields. This isn't necessarily a bad strategy if time proves them right. It wouldn't change our final result too much. What it would mean is that you'd just keep reinvesting the shorter-term matured bonds into new issues and hope the interest yields wouldn't dip below what the longer-term strips of today are offering.

"Second, you should be completely clear that if you lock into long-term strips, the yield you're going to get is precisely that—locked in. If inflation were to push up to 8 percent or more, and if bond yields rose to 12 percent or higher, naturally you wouldn't want to have all your money in instruments just keeping pace with inflation and netting you no gain. We believe bonds are safe instruments, and they are, but investors have to recognize the risks involved because of inflation and the direction of interest rates. To put it another way, do you go long term in the belief that interest rates are going to stay low, or do you go short, in the belief that rates are going to rise? Obviously you can do both, and this is what most advisers would recommend."

"We should add, too," Sara interposed, "that some people like to 'play' the strip-bond market. In our opinion, this defeats the whole purpose of bonds. If you mistime the market or the direction of interest rates, you can take a bath. For our purposes here, we'll just play it straight and view strip bonds as a simple strategy for deciding how much money you need for any given year in the future. Then we'd buy a strip bond today to produce the desired income, then. With strips you know up front:

- what you pay today,
- the interest yield, and
- the maturity value."

About Strips

"Strips are bonds without coupons," said Gordon, "so you don't see any interest until the bond actually matures. Brokerage houses offer high-quality strips issued by the federal and provincial governments and some Crown corporations. So the risk is negligible that you won't get paid when the bond matures. Of course, if the governments or corporations go broke there could be a problem, but if this happens it will also mean Canada's in a real mess! In that event, I'm not sure where your money would be any safer!

"Strip bonds work kind of in reverse. The issuer decides what sum of money a person needs to invest today to yield a certain value in 5, 10, 20, or even 30 years. This means you can buy a bond today for about $1,500 that will mature in 30 years and pay you $20,000 at that point. This approach makes long-term investing seem much more affordable, and it lets you plan your future income flows specifically and pretty securely.

"Bonds are good 'no brainer' investments that can give you peace of mind as long as you buy quality issues and don't change your mind and decide to cash them in early."

"No brainer," I said. "It does concern me a bit that they're the first approach you guys have decided to use with me."

"Yes, well, I wouldn't take it personally," Sara said. "We have strips in our portfolio, so you're in good company!"

Getting to Know the Steps

"Okay, suppose that, as of 1997, a person 45 years of age wants to retire in 2017. There are some simple steps he or she must take to determine what is best to do:

1. Decide how much annual income you'll need in 2017 and, of course, each year after that. To get these figures, use an inflation table. You want your annual income requirements to bear some semblance to your real costs in the future.

2. Now that we know roughly how much money you'll need to maintain a certain lifestyle in future years, we have to analyze how much money you currently have in RRSPs, other cashable assets, and all your other sources of future revenue.

3. If there is, or will be, enough money in your retirement portfolio to meet your future costs of living, you can relax and quit worrying. If, however, the future investment-growth figure doesn't measure up, it's time to plan strategies to ensure it does.

"For an easy example, let's suppose you need $20,000 to sustain the way you want to live in 2017. I know this figure is far too low given inflation. How much money do you need to put into a strip bond today to pay you $20,000 in 20 years?"

"You're the man with the calculator," I said.

"Well, I don't need the calculator for this—just the sheet of strip maturities and yields we used the other night."

He produced it again.

STRIP BOND COSTS AND MATURITY VALUES

Maturity Date	Investment Today	Yield (%)	Maturity Value
2011	$ 6,289	8.68	$ 20,000
2012	5,703	8.78	20,000
2013	5,162	8.89	20,000
2014	4,695	8.95	20,000
2015	4,338	8.95	20,000
2016	3,967	8.94	20,000
2017	3,797	8.68	20,000
2018	3,557	8.58	20,000
2019	3,243	8.66	20,000
2020	2,914	8.89	20,000
2021	2,846	8.39	20,000
2022	2,634	8.45	20,000
2023	2,400	8.52	20,000
2024	2,018	8.90	20,000
2025	1,865	8.87	20,000
2026	1,729	8.84	20,000
2027	1,702	8.56	20,000
2028	1,597	8.49	20,000
2029	1,571	8.43	20,000
2030	1,550	8.50	20,000
TOTAL	**$63,577**		**$400,000**

(Note: This table is provided for demonstration purposes only. While face values and interest yields were current at the time of writing, current purchase prices and yields change. Consult the appropriate institutions or financial advisers for current yields.)

"You can see that to guarantee a $20,000 payday in 2017, you need to put away only $3,797 today. So, that's year one of your retirement taken care of by stashing away less than $4,000. Now we can look at each year right up to 2030, when we see you'd need to commit only $1,550 today to get your $20,000.

"If we keep going like this, you can easily plan your income flow just by buying strip bonds with $20,000 maturity values. Invest $63,577 today and you'll realize maturity values of $400,000 over the 20 years from 2011 to 2030 (20 years x $20,000 per year).

"Many people have $63,577 in their self-directed RRSPs but they don't realize the true value of this sum of money. They look at it as a relatively small lump sum in today's dollars instead of as a substantial investment capable of reproducing like a rabbit over an extended period of time.

The Reluctant Millionaire

"I was at a dinner party last week where the subject of retirement came up. One of the people there lamented that he had only about $200,000 in his RRSP and therefore couldn't afford to retire in 12 years. I asked him what retirement income he thought this would produce. To my amazement he answered about $35,000 a year.

"He said he had arrived at this figure by calculating he'd contribute another $10,000 a year for 12 years, earn 6-percent interest per year, and that the whole sum would come to about $581,000 at the end of this time. He thought it reasonable to assume he could earn about a 6-percent return on that sum at the time of retirement. This is how he came up with the $35,000 in interest income. He hadn't really done anything wrong in his math, and he was aware that extracting all the interest each year would see the real value of his principal steadily eroded by inflation.

"He wasn't a happy fellow, but he looked at me like I was someone trying to raise capital for a risky gold mine when I told him he was sitting on more than a million dollars with just what he had in RRSPs now. I told him he could earn $60,000 a year for 19 years, beginning in 12 years, without saving another cent.

"You know, I invited him to call me so I could take just a couple of minutes to show him on paper what I meant, but I doubt he'll ever call. He'll just go on thinking his compounding $200,000 is worth only $35,000 a year. People spend hours trying to haggle over the price of a used car to save $500, but few want to spend ten minutes to learn how $200,000 is worth a million. I don't get it."

"I'll try to be a more appreciative student," I said. "In fact, with a bit of time to look this thing over, it does make sense because of the way you've broken down future years into individual annual segments. And you're right about something else, too. I haven't really thought about my investment time as being the rest of my life. I've been seeing it as only the years I have till retirement. We started saving late, like most people, but I see how even we can benefit from 30-plus years of compounding interest."

"Bravo, I'm making progress!" he said. "Let's keep going. Since we know $20,000 won't be nearly enough to live on in 2017, we have to double, triple, or quadruple the number of $20,000 strip bonds to produce $40,000 or $60,000 or $80,000 a year, or whatever income you feel will be necessary.

"From the foregoing table you can see that if we quadrupled the $63,577 investment and, instead, placed $254,308 in RRSP strip bonds today, we would get $80,000 a year for each of the 20 years. This adds up to $1,600,000 — a princely sum that you could have with no risk and with the strip interest yields returning less than 9 percent.

"The important point in all this," said Gordon, "is to start looking at your retirement as a series of year-to-year objectives instead of getting overwhelmed by: 'Oh, god, I've got to plan for 30 years and I need millions of dollars! I'll never get there, so I might as well buy that new stereo!'"

Saving by the yard is very hard.
Saving by the inch is a lead-pipe cinch.

*   *   *

"If you approach it year by year, using instruments as safe as strip bonds, you can make goals more achievable. For example, if you believe you need $80,000 to live on in 2017 and you have no other pension income, you know you just have to put $15,188 away today. And, if you're planning as far out as 2030, you need to contribute only $6,200 to get the $80,000. These numbers seem more real because they are within most people's grasp."

"So, what end of my retirement should I work on first?" I asked.

"I believe it makes the most sense to fill in your nearest retirement years first so your retirement horizon is in sight and secured. Then work back each successive year. The nice thing here is that it gets cheaper to do so because of the longer period of compounding and the less expensive face values of the strips today.

"Using this approach, and your existing $134,000 in RRSPs, you have the years 2017 to 2030 covered with an annual income of $80,000. We'll find out if this is enough in a little while, and then you'll know whether you have to:

- save more,
- fill in more years after 2030, because you'll only be 78, or
- if it looks as if you're going to be flush, try to move your retirement horizon up sooner than 2017.

Sara rejoined the conversation.

"It's comforting, isn't it, to see that even with instruments as safe as bonds you don't need the millions of dollars in an RRSP today, or even by the first year you retire? For people who didn't begin RRSPs until their mid-thirties or later, having million dollar-plus targets gets depressing because the goal seems impossible to reach."

Gordon had to prick her balloon.

"I should add, of course, that we haven't developed a picture yet of how much money you'll need once you retire. It's critical that we devote considerable effort to these projections. That said, I think it's time to get into some of the specifics of retirement planning. The good news is that it doesn't take a rocket scientist. If it did, I'd be of very little use to you."

"Right," I said. "I know I'm not planning interstellar flight, but it does seem to demand a lot of financial knowledge, and there are so many numbers about what you need to save, what you need in the future, how to get the most out of your investments. The list goes on and on. I get a headache just thinking about it."

"It's intimidating for most people," said Gordon, "but anyone with a cheap calculator who knows how to add, subtract, multiply, and divide can come up with a pretty decent financial plan in just a few hours. That's a small investment of time for something that'll benefit you for the rest of your life. Going through the process can also buy you peace of mind today. Many people have good retirement plans already under way and don't even know it!"

"Okay." I smiled. "I'll give you the benefit of the doubt. Where do I start?"

"Well, let's revisit the steps we mentioned just a while ago. We need to put numbers together on:

1. Income—now and projected into the future as best you can.
2. Cost-of-living data—now and projected into the future. Coming up with current costs is easy. Getting the ones we need for the future requires some thought about how you want to live your life in retirement. Then we work in an inflation factor to identify likely costs in the future.
3. Asset information—what assets do you have today and plan to have in the future that will affect your retirement finances? This includes work pensions, RRSPs, real estate, CPP, and so on.

4. How long do you have until retirement—the time you have to accumulate funds—and how long will these retirement funds have to last, given your probable life expectancy?"

"Sounds simple when you put it that way," I said, "but even my midget mathematical mind can see a lot of unknowns in there."

"Of course there are," said Gordon, "but that's no reason to avoid planning. You have to make best guesses, but if you pursue the approach we spoke of before—underestimate revenue and overestimate expenditures—that's the best you can do. It's a heck of a lot better than just throwing your hands in the air."

"Okay, okay, I concede," I said. "What next?"

Getting Down to Business

"Well, let's follow the four steps by figuring out your income and life budget today and in the future. Then we'll identify your assets to see if what you can accumulate will get the job done, and, if not, what steps you'll need to take to do it.

"I have a worksheet and an inflation factoring table to help us."

He handed me more sheets of paper and said, "I've given you two copies of each form. Complete one for your and Lorraine's situation now and take the extra copies home with you to photocopy for future use, and for any of your friends who might be interested.

"The first one is for income. You know what you both earn now. Just use the 2.5-percent inflation factor and we'll see where you'll be in 20 years."

"Well, there are a couple of wrinkles already," I said. "I'm self-employed and really don't know from year to year what I'm going to earn. As the old saying goes, 'when you're self-employed, you're always only three months from bankruptcy.' And Lorraine works for the province and there's word she could be a casualty of downsizing."

"Good point," said Gordon. "I'm glad you raised it. Many people don't know exactly what their income will be, and those who do are very fortunate. So, let's suppose yours will be considerably less in future than it has been in the past and that Lorraine also takes a cut in pay if she has to change jobs and winds up earning less. It's unlikely both situations would happen, but they could, and your planning should be for the worst case.

"What do you think are reasonable annual incomes for both of you, that you could probably sustain?"

"We're currently making about $70,000 a year between the two of us—what if we say $60,000?"

"Okay, let's go with that. What you have to do is start with your $60,000 combined and then inflate your incomes each year by assuming modest raises of 2.5 percent to keep pace with inflation; and then set aside your maximum RRSP contributions and compound them by a conservative rate of 6 percent.

"We'll assume you start this next year and that you'll both contribute your maximums up to and including the year 2016 and that you'll start your retirement on January 2, 2017."

FUTURE INCOME AND RRSP CONTRIBUTION PROJECTIONS

Assumptions:

a) That incomes inflate by 2.5% per year. Be conservative. Over-estimating will hurt!

b) That RRSP contribution limits will be raised from current levels in keeping with inflation and Canadians' higher earnings—calculate a consistent 18% contribution.

Column 1 shows the year. Column 2 indicates combined salary levels. Column 4 assumes the maximum RRSP contribution for the year, and column 6 shows how the annual contribution will grow, compounding at 6 % annually over a 20-year period.

Year	Combined Incomes	Salary Increase (%)	RRSP/ Year	RRSP Growth (%)	RRSP Value
1998	$60,000	2.50	$10,800	6.00	$11,448
1999	61,500	2.50	11,070	6.00	23,869
2000	63,038	2.50	11,347	6.00	37,329
2001	64,614	2.50	11,631	6.00	51,898
2002	66,229	2.50	11,921	6.00	67,648
2003	67,885	2.50	12,219	6.00	84,659
2004	69,582	2.50	12,525	6.00	103,015
2005	71,322	2.50	12,838	6.00	122,804
2006	73,105	2.50	13,159	6.00	144,121
2007	74,933	2.50	13,488	6.00	167,066
2008	76,806	2.50	13,825	6.00	191,744
2009	78,726	2.50	14,171	6.00	218,270
2010	80,694	2.50	14,525	6.00	246,763
2011	82,711	2.50	14,888	6.00	277,350
2012	84,779	2.50	15,260	6.00	310,167
2013	86,898	2.50	15,642	6.00	345,358
2014	89,070	2.50	16,033	6.00	383,074
2015	91,297	2.50	16,433	6.00	423,477
2016	93,579	2.50	16,844	6.00	466,740

FUTURE INCOME AND RRSP CONTRIBUTION PROJECTIONS

Worksheet assumptions:

a) That current income(s) inflate by 2.5% per year. Be conservative. Overestimating will hurt!

b) That RRSP contribution limits will be raised from current levels in keeping with inflation and Canadians' higher earnings—calculate a consistent 18% contribution.

Year	Combined Incomes	RRSP (18% of Taxable Income)	Compounded @ 6%
1998	$	$	$
1999			
2000			
2001			
2002			
2003			
2004			
2005			
2006			
2007			
2008			
2009			
2010			
2011			
2012			
2013			
2014			
2015			
2016			
2017			
2018			
2019			
2020			
2021			
2022			
2023			
2024			
2025			
2026			
2027			

It took me a few minutes to calculate the income and RRSP projections. Then I got to work figuring out our costs of living as they were today and trying to guess intelligently how much they would increase over a 20-year period. I made some of my own assumptions along the way:

- We would have no mortgage or loans outstanding when we retired.
- We could stop saving for retirement at age 65.
- We would have no dependents.
- Lorraine and I planned to get rid of one motor vehicle in retirement because the cost of running two would be excessive.
- I thought we'd dine out a lot more, even when at home by ordering in.
- We planned to spend three months a year outside Canada, and it seemed a safe bet that costs for travel, accommodation, and food would be quite high. I made "best guesses."
- The 7-percent miscellaneous addition seemed logical to me since it's impossible to account for every dollar spent every month.

ANNUAL COST-OF-LIVING WORKSHEET—NOW AND THEN

It's impossible to plan your retirement if you don't project the way you hope to live in the future. For most people this means continuing life as usual for much of the year—without the job, of course. The "blip" in the picture becomes the money you'll need for recreation and travel.

To project how much you'll need, try to put some "annual" figures into the categories on the blank worksheet on the following page. You can calculate the all-important inflation factor from the table that follows.

	Cost Today ($)	Inflation Factor	Cost at Retirement ($)
Mortgage/Rent	4,800	1.64	0
Property taxes	4,000	1.64	6,560
Home insurance	500	1.64	820
Maintenance	400	1.64	656
Utilities	2,400	1.64	3,936
Debts/Loans	2,000	-	0
Retirement savings	10,000	-	0
Education costs	0	-	0
Family expenses	0	-	0
Groceries	6,000	1.64	9,840
Life insurance	0	-	0
Health-care costs	300	-	1,200
Motor vehicle(s)			
—Gas	1,800	1/2 @ 1.64	1,476
—Insurance	2,200	1/2 @ 1.64	1,804
—Maintenance	300	1.64	492
—Boat/RV	0	-	0
Clothing	600	1.64	984
Home			
—Sports	300	1.64	492
—Recreation	300	1.64	492
—Dining out	600	-	1,800
Holidays			
—Airfare	600	-	1,640
—By vehicle	300	1.64	492
—Accommodation	500	-	14,760
—Food/Dining	1,000	-	5,000
—Sports	300	-	1,000
—Recreation	500	-	2,000
—Other	300	-	1,000
Other:_____	0	-	0
Misc. (7% of total)	2,800	-	3,951
TOTAL	**$42,800**	-	**$60,395**

ANNUAL COST-OF-LIVING WORKSHEET—NOW AND THEN

	Cost Today ($)	Inflation Factor	Cost at Retirement($)
Mortgage/Rent	_____	_____	_____
Property taxes	_____	_____	_____
Home insurance	_____	_____	_____
Maintenance	_____	_____	_____
Utilities	_____	_____	_____
Debts/Loans	_____	_____	_____
Retirement savings	_____	_____	_____
Education costs	_____	_____	_____
Family expenses	_____	_____	_____
Groceries	_____	_____	_____
Life insurance	_____	_____	_____
Health-care costs	_____	_____	_____
Motor vehicle(s)			
—Gas	_____	_____	_____
—Insurance	_____	_____	_____
—Maintenance	_____	_____	_____
—Boat/RV	_____	_____	_____
Clothing	_____	_____	_____
Home			
—Sports	_____	_____	_____
—Recreation	_____	_____	_____
—Dining out	_____	_____	_____
Holidays			
—Airfare	_____	_____	_____
—By vehicle	_____	_____	_____
—Accommodation	_____	_____	_____
—Food/Dining	_____	_____	_____
—Sports	_____	_____	_____
—Recreation	_____	_____	_____
—Other	_____	_____	_____
Other:_____	_____	_____	_____
Misc. (7% of total)	_____	_____	_____
TOTAL	_____	_____	_____

INFLATION FACTOR TABLE

No one can predict precisely what inflation will be in the coming decades, but it is important to make an educated guess so future income needs are as accurate as possible. Given the current economic climate, and the fact that governments in Canada and the U.S. are committed to controlling inflation, inflation could well remain at current levels for some time. No one wants a return to the days of high inflation, and manufacturers, labor unions, and the population in general have reduced expectations considerably from what they were in the 1980s.

We've used 2.5% as our inflation rate in this table.

Using the Table

1. Calculate the number of years you want to project into the future, and
2. Multiply the cost of something today by the inflation factor.

For example, if something costs $100 today and you want to project what it will cost in 25 years, multiply $100 x 1.85 and you know you should plan to pay $185 at that time.

No. of years to project	Inflation factor @ 2.5%	No. of years to project	Inflation factor @ 2.5%
1	1.03	19	1.60
2	1.05	20	1.64
3	1.08	21	1.68
4	1.10	22	1.72
5	1.13	23	1.76
6	1.16	24	1.81
7	1.19	25	1.85
8	1.22	26	1.90
9	1.25	27	1.95
10	1.28	28	2.00
11	1.31	29	2.05
12	1.34	30	2.10
13	1.38	31	2.15
14	1.41	32	2.20
15	1.45	33	2.26
16	1.48	34	2.32
17	1.52	35	2.37
18	1.56	36	2.43

After I'd completed the cost-of-living form, Gordon examined it for a couple of minutes.

"Okay, that looks pretty complete. It gives us very useful information. Your future needs don't bear a lot of resemblance to your current needs since you plan to live out of the country for one quarter of the year. But now we know you should plan for $60,395 net income in the first year of your retirement. If we assume that's evenly split between you and Lorraine, the annual net is about $30,200.

"Since people pay both federal and provincial tax and tax rates vary according to the province, we'll keep our calculations simple. Let's assume you'll each pay a combined federal and provincial tax rate of about 30 percent. That means your gross must be $43,139 each, or $86,278 a year combined. We should start dealing with gross taxable income since you'll have to pay taxes on the proceeds taken from your RRSPs.

(Note: This 30-percent tax rate used in the foregoing illustration approximates the combined federal and provincial tax rates for the income level given as of 1996. You should verify current tax rates for your individual income and according to the province in which you reside. See table following for 1996 rates.)

1996 FEDERAL INCOME TAX RATES

Taxable Income	Tax
$0–$29,590	17% (i.e., $5,030 on $29,590)
$29,590–$59,180	17% + 26% (i.e., $5,030 + $7,693 on next $29,590 = $12,723)
$59,180+	17% + 26% + 29% (i.e., $12,723 + 29% thereafter)

1996 PROVINCIAL INCOME TAX RATES

Percentage of Federal Tax

Alberta	45.5	N.W.T	45.0
B.C.	52.0	Ontario	56.0
Manitoba	52.0	P.E.I.	59.5
New Brunswick	64.0	Quebec	N/A
Nfld.	69.0	Sask.	50.0
Nova Scotia	59.5	Yukon	50.0

"Yikes!" I said. "The tax hit is huge."

"Actually, it gets worse," said Gordon. "If we take the $86,278 figure and assume you both live 20 more years after that, the annual gross income needs mushroom to $141,376—that's $70,688 each."

"But that's impossible!" I said. "The way this is going, it doesn't look like we'll ever be able to live the lifestyle we want to."

"Hold on, don't start getting depressed yet. It *is* likely that you can influence the outcomes by making some choices."

"What choices and what outcomes?"

FINANCIAL PLANNING IS ABOUT MAKING CHOICES

"Well," said Gordon. "You have some clear choices:

- put more money away before retirement,
- reduce your retirement living expenses,
- reduce your retirement holiday expectations, or
- spend really fast for a few years and die young."

I frowned.

"I don't like any of your options. The first one we can probably do if we get even more serious about saving, but how do I reduce my retirement living expenses without sacrificing quality of life?"

"You do what we've done," he said.

"It doesn't look to me like you guys have sacrificed much."

"No, we haven't. We just do some things a bit differently, things that cost less but that aren't necessarily a big sacrifice. I can see some ways to save you money very easily."

"I suppose you're going to want a cut of the savings?"

"Well, only a small one. If I can save you $3,000 in three minutes and if you agree that making the savings would be no big sacrifice, how about buying a nice bottle of Châteauneuf for supper?"

"Deal!"

"Okay, let's look at your needs for the year 2017. It makes sense that your mortgage will be gone, but it looks to me as if you're still paying property taxes for a home in the city. Move to a retirement village in a less expensive area and you can cut those taxes to about $400 per month in 2017 dollars—that's $1,760 saved.

"With the move to a smaller house come savings in utilities. You're paying $200 a month now. Cut your living area in half, from 2,500 square feet to 1,250 square feet, be careful with your insulation and the heating system, and you can cut that monthly bill by $100 in today's dollars. Inflate that $100 by the 1.64 factor and you get $164 per month, or $1,968 per year in 2017. That cuts $1,968 from your projection of annual utilities expenses. How'm I doing? By my calculations I've just saved you $3,728 net a year. Just as important, that net reduces your gross by $5,326. Now you only need to have an income of $80,952. Do I get my bottle of wine?"

"Sure," I said. "Can you buy Châteauneuf for five dollars? With the money I'll have to put aside, I can no longer afford the good stuff."

Gordon chuckled.

"Don't be cheap. You can start saving more when you get home. We're just poor retired folk who can't afford good wine ourselves. Besides, maybe you'll feel better when I tell you how to save even more money."

"You want the wine before you'll tell me more?"

"No," he said, "but I would like the $20 it'll cost."

"Okay, here's your kickback. Tell me more."

"Right," said Gordon. "There are some little things you should know about. How much they benefit you depends on how much work you're willing to put into finding yourself deals. For example, retired people usually save money, or can save money, through:

- lower real estate taxes through government grants;
- discounts for retired people;
- the need for fewer acquisitions, owing to your real estate downsizing and the simple fact that retirees seem to "consume" less and choose instead to "do" more;
- being diligent about your travel expenditures. If you stick to the heavily traveled tourist routes, you'll pay through the nose. But I don't think it would take too much effort and thought to trim your five-star travel budget.

"More about possible savings later," said Gordon. "For now, I'd like to keep going on your sources of income so we can assemble a complete picture of how much money you're likely to have."

Completing the Income Stream

"You like worst-case scenarios, so for the sake of argument, let's look at the rosiest picture. This projection does require that you make some important changes in your life. Specifically, it means selling your house before you retire, perhaps renting for a while and then, once you retire, moving to a less expensive area to live in, we hope, just as nice a house as the one you have now, at lower cost. Doing precisely this hasn't struck us as a sacrifice at all."

House Sale Adds to Compounding Years

"When you contemplate cashing in a house in favor of a retirement cottage, consider several factors:

1. Where is the house located?
2. What will its value likely be a few years before you retire?
3. What will it cost you to buy land and build a retirement cottage for yourself somewhere else?

"Obviously the cashing-out concept won't work for everyone. It's not a great option for someone who owns a home in an area where real estate prices are depressed, particularly if buying a new residence in the desired retirement location would mean spending *more* money. But for many Canadians it's going to be possible to cash out of urban centers where real estate values remain relatively high and move to more rural locations where land prices are much lower. Some cities and areas where prices will probably stay high are B.C.'s Lower Mainland, the Toronto and Ottawa areas, and B.C.'s Okanagan. Several million Canadians will be able to take advantage of this cashing-out option.

"Even now, we're seeing news features occasionally about future retirement destinations in rural Canada that were considered totally out of the way and quite undesirable just five years ago.

"I believe that even someone who owns a modest $100,000 home in Montreal, Calgary, Saskatoon, or Winnipeg could move to a retirement community, say one specializing in manufactured or mobile homes, bank a good sum of money and significantly reduce monthly expenses. You can buy a very nice, almost new, manufactured home today for $45,000, get a fully serviced lot in a cooperative living community for $25,000, and be fully set up for $70,000 in total. This would let you bank $30,000 and cut living expenses like heating bills, property taxes, and so on to save maybe $300 a month. The interest on the $30,000 plus the $3,600 in annual savings could become a nice sum of extra disposable cash every year for quite a few years.

"But, since you and a couple of million other Canadians live in the Lower Mainland and Vancouver Island, let's look at prices from there. The average house price in the Lower Mainland is now about $300,000, right? Given the continuing influx of people from the rest of Canada and from other countries, it isn't much of a stretch to figure that the average price there will be about $400,000 in 10 to 15 years. Let's assume you're willing to sell your house and can replace it with something smaller and cheaper away from the maddening crowd—say a nice little cottage for $250,000. You could bank the excess $150,000. Look at what that could do for you."

"What?" I asked.

"Well, the sale of your principal residence would give you the $150,000 tax-free, but the interest on this money would be taxable. Conversely, the interest compounding in your RRSPs would be tax-sheltered. So, it would make sense to spend the house capital and leave your RRSPs to continue to grow. We know you need about $86,000 plus or minus gross and that you'll get about $28,000 from CPP and Lorraine's pension, so the house capital would totally top up your first two years of income needs and part of a third. All this time your RRSPs are quietly growing, and pretty darn quickly, too.

"For the sake of discussion, let's see what you could have if you were willing to act on this strategy. First, we'll look at year 2017:

1. You'll have the $150,000 of house capital that we'll draw down each year as needed and until it's gone to add to your CPP and Lorraine's superannuation pension.
2. If you have the house sale proceeds, you can start your strip bonds maturing in the year 2019 instead of 2017. This makes them even less expensive for you to purchase *now*. I think we'll see you getting $80,000 per year for quite a few years beginning in 2019.

3. There's $22,704 per year in combined income for you and Lorraine from CPP, which starts coming to you in 2017. This estimate is based on today's maximum entitlement of $713 inflated by 1.5 percent a year for 20 years.
4. You'll have $5,000 per year from Lorraine's superannuation.
5. All during these first years, the interest will still be growing in your RRSPs. We won't start taking anything out, over and above the strip bonds, until we need to either get your income to where you need it to be, or to satisfy the government's RRIF draw-down requirements, which kick in when you turn 69. You'll start with $466,741 in 2017 if you max your contributions over the next 20 years.
6. A question mark is how much, if any, money you can earn from your retirement business. Let's assume zero right now.

"So, it's already clear that you can have the income you believe you'll need. All it requires is that you keep doing what you've been doing and sell your house to free up capital at some point over the next decade.

"We'll have to see what happens with the numbers. It'll be interesting to see if you have a surplus in your later years or a deficit. Our own investments will be pretty much run down by the time we're in our mid-eighties, and although we might live to be 100, we don't consider that too likely. I think people who think they're going to live to be centenarians are most likely going to die with a lot of money in the bank for their heirs or the government. We intend to spend ours on ourselves.

"As I mentioned, you also have to factor in that the government requires you to start running down your RRIF when you turn 69, so our choice to spend most of our money by age 85 doesn't deviate much from what they would force us to do, anyway.

"But I digress. Let's see how much money *you're* going to need for things to work out from the time you retire in 2017 to 2042, when you'll be 90 years old. With these projections we'll

then have clear targets against which to match your income flow.
I think another table is in order."

Gordon poked for a few minutes to produce:

INCOME PROJECTIONS FOR YEARS 2017–2042

Assumes an inflation rate of 2.5% per year

Year	Income Need with Inflation Adjustment	Year	Income Need with Inflation Adjustment
2017	$ 86,278	2030	$118,935
2018	88,435	2031	121,908
2019	90,646	2032	124,956
2020	92,912	2033	128,080
2021	95,235	2034	131,282
2022	97,616	2035	134,564
2023	100,056	2036	137,928
2024	102,557	2037	141,376
2025	105,121	2038	144,910
2026	107,749	2039	148,533
2027	110,443	2040	152,246
2028	113,204	2041	156,052
2029	116,034	2042	159,954

"Now we have a pretty good idea of what you'll need to maintain the lifestyle you've chosen," said Gordon. "I think that in
reality you may not spend as much on travel in your advanced
age, but you may well have to spend more on health care or on
help to maintain your house and yourselves, so it's good to keep
estimates on the high side."

PUTTING IT ALL TOGETHER

"The question now is, do you have, or can you put together, what you'll need to do it?

"We'll have to do the calculations, but the good news is that starting in 2017 you have your house capital, CPP, and Lorraine's superannuation pension. We also know your strips won't cut in until about 2019 and will pay out $80,000 for quite a few years without your having to touch your other RRSP funds at all.

"If your needs can be met using the house, strips, CPP, and Lorraine's pension for a few years before you start running down your remaining RRIF, your situation may come out all right. We assume, again, that you earn 6-percent interest on the remaining principal, and that CPP and Lorraine's pension continue to grow by a modest 1.5 percent per year.

"I would also suggest you and Lorraine take advantage now of a bonus that you can have at some point in your retirement by using up your $2,000 RRSP overcontributions. If you use that $4,000 now, you can secure another $40,000 income in 2024 strips by buying two for about $4,000 now. We won't factor this in, but I think it would be a very good strategic move if you can swing it.

"It's also obvious that you're going to earn more money than you need in the early years from your matured strips and CPP. For our planning purposes, we'll show the excess as 'cumulative after-tax excess.' Depending on what comes out, you could either decide to spend more by living a slightly more expensive lifestyle in your early retirement years, or play it conservatively and let this surplus build up in case you need special health care at some point later in your lives."

Minimum RRIF Withdrawals

"Now's a good time to cover that RRIF draw-down wrinkle Ottawa throws at you when you turn 69. The schedule of minimum withdrawals is as follows, and we'll have to add to your income whenever, or if ever, it falls short of the RRIF minimum draw-downs. Of course, if you don't need the extra money, you don't have to spend it; the government just doesn't want it tax-sheltered anymore. It may be wise to save it outside the RRIF for later years if one, or both, of you live to be a centenarian. You may also need it for higher health-care expenses.

"Since you'll have $80,000 in maturing strip bonds for the first few years of your retirement, you may not have to touch your principal from your other RRSPs, and the RRIF draw-down percentages may not require that you take anything other than your strip proceeds. We'll see.

RRIF DRAW-DOWN SCHEDULE, STARTING AT AGE 69

Age	Percentage	Age	Percentage
69	7.38	81	9.58
70	7.48	82	9.93
71	7.59	83	10.33
72	7.71	84	10.79
73	7.85	85	11.33
74	7.99	86	11.96
75	8.15	87	12.71
76	8.33	88	13.62
77	8.53	89	14.73
78	8.75	90	16.12
79	8.99	91	17.92
80	9.27	92+ each year thereafter	20.00

(Note: Check with Revenue Canada for most recent RRIF draw-down formulas)

"So, let's see where the numbers take us. I know these tables look complicated with so many numbers, but if you look across the page at a single year at a time, you'll see there are only 11 pieces of information.

"It takes a while to do such a projection, but a couple of hours spent doing this can help keep you focused for many years. I should also add that everyone's situation will look different. The table we're working up for you is easily adapted to other people's needs as long as they have some idea of income flows and costs of living and where pension plans are *likely* to end up—some speculative guesswork to be sure, but there's no way around it if you want a plan.

"At any rate, what we have in your table is 11 columns that tell us the following:

1. Your ages—both of you will turn 65 early in 2017.
2. The corresponding year.
3. The compounding principal value of your RRSP/RRIF funds, to which you'll contribute for the next 20 years.
4. The drawing down of the $150,000 you net from selling your city home.
5. Combined "before tax" payment from CPP and Lorraine's pension.
6. The value of your matured strip bonds beginning in 2019 with the last one maturing in 2038.
7. How much money must be drawn out of your RRIF to meet government minimums.
8. Your house capital draw-down for the first three years to reach your projected income needs.
9. Your total income for the given year.
10. Our estimate of what you will actually need in these years, given your preferred lifestyle and building in the 2.5-percent annual inflation calculation.
11. The build-up of any excess.

INCOME PROJECTIONS

Assumes 6% Interest on RRSP Savings, 30% Income Taxes on House Capital Interest
Assumes 1.5% Growth on CPP and Pension

Age	Year	Compounding RRSP/RRIF Funds	House Capital	CPP & Pension Income	Strip Bond RRSP/RRIF Income	Additional RRIF Draw-down	House Capital Draw-down	Total Income	Required Income	Cumulative After Tax Excess
65	2017	$466,741	$150,000	$27,704	$0	$0	$58,574	$86,278	$86,278	$0
66	2018	494,745	95,266	28,120	0	0	60,315	88,435	88,435	0
67	2019	524,430	36,419	28,542	80,000	0	36,419	144,961	90,646	32,589
68	2020	555,896	0	28,970	80,000	0	0	108,970	92,912	43,397
69	2021	589,250	0	29,405	80,000	0	0	109,405	95,235	53,461
70	2022	624,605	0	29,846	80,000	0	0	109,846	97,616	62,724
71	2023	662,081	0	30,294	80,000	0	0	110,294	100,056	71,125
72	2024	701,806	0	30,748	80,000	22,983	0	133,731	102,557	92,390
73	2025	720,931	0	31,209	80,000	23,841	0	135,050	105,121	113,673
74	2026	740,346	0	31,677	80,000	24,670	0	136,347	107,749	134,924
75	2027	760,097	0	32,152	80,000	25,449	0	137,601	110,443	156,076
76	2028	780,254	0	32,634	80,000	26,290	0	138,924	113,204	177,127
77	2029	800,779	0	33,124	80,000	26,886	0	140,010	116,034	197,889
78	2030	821,940	0	33,621	80,000	27,489	0	141,110	118,935	218,318
79	2031	843,767	0	34,125	80,000	28,057	0	142,182	121,908	238,342

Age	Year	Compounding RRSP/RRIF Funds	House Capital	CPP & Pension Income	Strip Bond RRSP/RRIF Income	Additional RRIF Draw-down	House Capital Draw-down	Total Income	Required Income	Cumulative After Tax Excess
80	2032	$866,336	$0	$34,637	$80,000	$28,539	$0	$143,176	$124,956	257,854
81	2033	889,777	0	35,157	80,000	28,886	0	144,043	128,080	276,715
82	2034	914,278	0	35,684	80,000	29,044	0	144,728	131,282	294,744
83	2035	940,091	0	36,219	80,000	29,191	0	145,410	134,564	311,862
84	2036	967,305	0	36,762	80,000	29,108	0	145,870	137,928	327,854
85	2037	996,235	0	37,313	80,000	28,819	0	146,132	141,376	342,510
86	2038	1,027,190	0	37,873	21,000	87,314	0	146,187	144,910	355,607
87	2039	1,001,507	0	38,441	0	110,092	0	148,533	148,533	368,409
88	2040	951,505	0	39,018	0	113,228	0	152,246	152,246	381,672
89	2041	895,367	0	39,603	0	116,449	0	156,052	156,052	395,412
90	2042	832,640	0	40,197	0	119,756	0	159,953	159,953	409,647
91	2043	762,842	0	40,800	0	123,154	0	163,954	163,952	424,395
92	2044	685,459	0	41,412	0	126,641	0	168,053	168,051	439,674
93	2045	599,946	0	42,033	0	130,222	0	172,255	172,252	455,504
94	2046	505,721	0	42,663	0	133,898	0	176,561	176,558	471,905
95	2047	402,166	0	43,303	0	137,672	0	180,975	180,972	488,897

Note: Anyone with a calculator or a computer spreadsheet program can replicate a similar table very easily. Alternatively, ask a financial adviser to create one to reflect your situation.

*   *   *

Gordon calculated for about half an hour.

"Well," he said finally, sitting back to look at the sheet for a few minutes. "That's interesting, isn't it?

"We have you both to 90 years of age with considerable funds remaining. If this works out to be accurate, you'd face some nice options: spend more sooner, save the money in case of some unforeseen event, or perhaps do a bit of both. Not a bad position to be in. You may even be able to retire a year or so earlier!"

Gordon looked pleased the picture had worked out positively. "You seem to have the option to have the income you'd need to live the lifestyle you want in your retirement.

"It seems a safe assumption that the three months of travel will probably cease as you near your eighties, but these funds may well go to increased medical or care expenses at that point.

"And, there are still at least three unknowns we haven't even factored into our calculations:

1. Funds you save over the next 15 years outside your RRSP—this could be an additional $100,000-plus if you can put away $5,000 each year;
2. Income you can earn in retirement from your business(es); and
3. Other assets you could cash in.

I thought for a moment.

"Okay, you've covered the house, but what other assets could we cash in?"

"Well, I'm not sure, but many people have others that aren't really necessary in the big picture. What are your other major assets?"

"The only other things we have that are worth much are our vehicles."

"And they are?"

"Lorraine has a Nissan Pathfinder and I drive a Volvo."

"Are they new?"

"Yes, pretty much—one or two years old."

"How much money do you have tied up in them?"

"Altogether? About $65,000."

"Do you think you could get by on less expensive vehicles? A little serious looking can turn up pretty good transportation for $10,000 at the most. What could you sell them for?"

"Probably $40,000 to $45,000."

"So, if you could get two older, but still good, vehicles for $20,000, you'd free up at least $20,000. I'm not saying you should do this, but you have a lot of money tied up in depreciating assets. Do you think it's really necessary? Imagine what that extra $20,000 could do over the next two decades, and ask yourselves if driving something a bit less expensive would really cramp your styles or damage your Yuppie images."

"Well, it's certainly something to think about," I said, my mind whirring.

Knock Off a Year Earlier

"Let me put that $20,000 into a context that might mean more to you. You've heard of the Rule of 72, I imagine?"

"No, I haven't."

"Okay, well it's something you should keep in the back of your mind for doing quick fiscal calculations. The Rule of 72 enables you to calculate easily how long it takes a given sum of money to double. All you do is divide 72 by the percentage return you can get on an investment. For example, let's suppose you could get 8 percent a year for the $20,000 freed up by selling your new vehicles. Divide eight into 72 and you get nine, correct? Well, that's how long it will take to double your $20,000 to $40,000. Do you see the possibilities?"

"I see the possibility of liking $40,000 twice as much as I would $20,000," I said.

"You're a linear thinker," he said with a hint of exasperation in his voice.

"If your $20,000 becomes $40,000 in nine years, the $40,000 becomes $80,000 in 18 years. We've already calculated that $80,000 is pretty close to what you need in gross income to live for a year, and 18 years is two years before your selected retirement date. It looks to me as if selling those cars and investing the money could let you knock off a year earlier for sure."

Suddenly my pampered black Volvo 850 lost some of its luster.

"Even allowing that we've thrown a lot of information and options at you and I understand, as well, that you can plan yourself into a pretzel, your situation looks pretty darn good. It probably mirrors that of a lot of other boomers who think they're destitute, too, simply because they haven't taken the time to do all the calculations. Also they fail to use the years after retirement to continue to build their capital."

I stared at the numbers for several minutes. Surely there was something wrong here. I had presumed for several years that there were big problems with our retirement prospects and now in only a few hours these friends had produced something in black and white that was doable and relatively painless. I must have been grinning like an idiot because both Gordon and Sara burst out laughing.

"You've heard about the cat and the mouse and the cheese," said Sara. "Well, we can tell you're not seeing yourself as the cheese!"

"Yes," I replied. "I have to admit I didn't expect this at all. I'm still having some trouble believing it. We've been looking at our $134,000 RRSPs as pretty paltry, but the way you've laid it out makes a lot of sense. I just had never approached the concept systematically. Damn! Here I've been working on an ulcer that isn't even necessary!"

"Well, if we've helped you avoid that, our time has been really worthwhile," said Gordon. "Maybe I should ask for another $20 for two bottles of wine while you're in such a good mood."

"Hey, relax, fiscal gurus. I think I'd better start saving now so I can build up our non-RRSP reserves."

"Looks like we've created a monster, Gord," said Sara. "Not that I think you're really serious, Richard, but given your newfound position of millionaire-in-waiting, you should keep an old saying in mind: 'The pursuit of prosperity need not be an unworthy goal. But an excess of it often changes one's values, and its actual attainment is very dangerous to many people.'

"Point taken," I said. "My values aren't about to change. The one thing I would value right now is some free time. We've been at this all day and my brain hurts."

"God, you're right!" said Sara. "It's almost four o'clock. We have to pick up Cosmo and get going."

"Where are we going?" I asked.

"Down the lake three miles for a visit with some other friends, Doug and Sheena Martini. They're having a dinner party with some interesting people we want you to meet. They have some different perspectives on how to ensure comfortable retirements that we think you should hear about. Most of them are quite well off from doing different things. We'll see what you think."

Work consists of whatever a body is *obliged* to do, and Play consists of whatever a body is not obliged to do.

— Mark Twain

CHAPTER 4

Do What
You Do Best

Chapter Goal: To demonstrate how traditional RRSP savings strategies may not work for entrepreneurs who often have erratic or low taxable incomes. There are other ways to secure a comfortable retirement for people in this position.

DAY 2, Evening

It took us only a few minutes to change and make our way to Cosmo's house. It and the yard had a decided Oriental flair. Bamboo grew in profusion and a lit stone lantern and stoic, moss-encrusted Buddha flanked the entry walk. More moss carpeted the flagstones. The pathway wound around a small reflecting pond dappled with water lilies. The front door opened before we knocked.

He looked only about 50, yet Gordon had told me he was at least 65. His face was lined, apparently from the sun and the time he spent outdoors rather than his age. His posture was confidently erect, his upper body tapered to a narrow waist, and his eyes were alert, bright and smiling. I liked him immediately.

"Cosmo, meet our good friend Richard, the big-city fellow we've been telling you about."

"Hi, Richard," he said, extending a callused hand. His grip was firm and warm. "Come in, please. Have we time for a little sake before we go?"

"Sure, what the hay. It'll only take us a few minutes to get there."

The house's interior matched its exterior, Spartan and tasteful, and continuing the Eastern theme through its art and furnishings. Comfortable and utilitarian. If I suspended reality, I could imagine myself in Japan.

"You like sake, Richard?" he asked.

"Yes, thank you. One of our favorite outings in the city is for Japanese food."

He disappeared for a moment. I took the opportunity to read another of those burl plaques that Cosmo made and gave to friends all over the Last Resort. This one, Gordon told me, pretty much summed up Cosmo's philosophy of life:

> Think about the negativism of the 10 commandments brought down from the mountain. Of the 10 commandments, seven are things people "must not do." Only three are things "to do." Consider the world that might have been if churches had taught compassion instead of fear. How about a rewrite—14 Paths for Life:

1. Value time.
2. Take pride in successes that come from perseverance.
3. View work as pleasure.
4. Honor the dignity of simplicity.
5. Know the worth of character.
6. Understand the power of reciprocity and kindness.
7. Strive to set a good example for others.
8. Meet the obligations of duty.
9. Appreciate the wisdom of economy.
10. Practice the virtue of patience.
11. Rejoice at the improvement of talent.

12. Cherish the joy of originality.
13. Respect all life forms.
14. Cultivate a lifelong love of learning.

—Anonymous

Cosmo returned with a square black tray. Arranged symmetrically in its center were four small, white porcelain cups circling a taller vessel, its narrow mouth giving vent to a slender tendril of steam.

Cosmo poured carefully and handed each of us a glass. Then, hoisting his own in salute, he toasted: "To the whetstone."

We all hesitated and then mimicked, almost in unison, "To the whetstone."

Cosmo burst into laughter. "Isn't anyone going to ask what the hell I'm talking about?"

Gordon volunteered.

"Okay, I'll bite, although I should know by now that this is probably another one of your off-colored perversions of some sage proverb."

"I'm wounded," said Cosmo. "This toast is in honor of Richard."

More blank looks from the three of us.

"Let me explain," he said. "You told me Richard is here, at least in part, to pick your brains about your retirement plan— excuse me, your detirement plan! Well, it might help if I complete the proverb: "The whetstone is dull, but it serves to sharpen the blade.""

"That's great," said Gordon, smiling.

"I'm not finished," said Cosmo. "You're too much of a linear thinker, my friend. Does it make more sense if you envision yourselves as the whetstones, the slightly used and dulled instruments, serving to hone the knowledge of the younger?"

"Thanks a lot!" exclaimed Sara. "I'm not sure I like being compared to a dull rock."

Cosmo gave her an endearing smile.

"Oh, you're anything but a dull rock. A rock is a dumb object, whereas a whetstone is a very useful thing. Time-worn maybe, but quite beautiful."

"You've got a real weird way with compliments, Cosmo," she said delivering a solid jab to his arm. "I'll accept the beautiful with thanks, but I'll have to think more about the time-worn part."

We finished the rice wine, our talk continuing its good-humored tone. Cosmo must be fun at a party. I'd expected someone monk-like. Still, I suspected he had layers of personality that would take time to penetrate. Sara had told me he'd never married, for example, yet he was very popular with women whenever he encountered them. The charming, solitary samurai.

Too soon we finished our drinks and had to go. We headed down to the boat.

Once out of dock Gordon steered west into the sun. Cosmo sat in a lotus position in the bow, rough cotton shirt open to his navel and wind whipping his shoulder-length hair. The image reminded me of *Apocalypse Now*, with its competent and eccentric Vietnam veteran. Good guy to have along, I thought, if Kootenay Lake harbored any modern-day pirates. Sara and I sat in the stern, so I asked her about the evening ahead.

"Okay. A quick rundown. They're all quite successful in their own rights. You'll be interested to know that none of them is following the type of retirement planning concepts we've outlined for you. I think you'll find that they've devised their retirement strategies based on entrepreneurship. This approach works for them and it's pretty hard to fault their successes."

"Do you mean they don't believe in RRSPs and pension plans?" I asked.

"Not really," said Sara. "I have to say we don't subscribe to this approach for 99 percent of the people we can think of, either. Many would just use nonsaving as a way to procrastinate. Others might delude themselves into thinking they can plot a successful retirement without deliberately putting away pension savings and then find out, too late, that they were wrong.

"These people don't seem to be wrong, though. They're all a lot fiscally smarter than your average birds. They have specific strengths and knowledge that position them well to make money without focusing too much on RRSPs.

"I'll give you some details on the cast of players.

"The hosts, Doug and Sheena, own a very profitable hotel that promises to provide them with a very healthy retirement income. They have trained such good staff that they now feel comfortable in semi-retirement having their bonus checks sent to Hawaii, or wherever they choose to vacation. They're in the enviable position of being able to keep the business and make money without working too much, or selling it someday when they don't want to be bothered working at all.

"You'll also meet Russ and Barb Waters. Russ is a realtor who found he could do better investing his RRSP savings in real estate. He knows the marketplace and he's good at spotting properties that'll return profits far exceeding what we've been able to manage in bonds, stocks, and mutual funds. He actually had quite a bit of money in RRSPs, but the returns paled in comparison to his other investments, so he's really not too enthusiastic about them anymore.

"The Waterses bought a piece of lake property in the Rockies that they're turning into a retirement village. You can probably get some good information from them about how they're proceeding with that.

"Then, there're Gerard Rothram and Larissa Labont. They own an investment-counseling firm. They're prime examples of people who saw a growth market and decided to capitalize on the investment scramble created by you boomers as you rush to sock away your retirement funds. They have RRSPs—it would look really strange if investment counselors didn't—but I think it's a safe bet that their business will net them a small fortune by the time they're ready to retire, and the RRSPs will be secondary."

"Okay," I said, "that's Doug, Sheba, Russ, Barb, Gerard, and Larissa." I always hated trying to memorize names at the time of the handshakes, my mind always goes blank.

"Very good," said Sara, "except it's Sheena, not Sheba. She may not mind being likened to the ancient queen, but they have a cute little dog named Sheba so you might not want to make that faux pas or you may find yourself eating on the porch!"

"Thanks! So you're telling me that all these people are ignoring the traditional ways of saving for retirement because they're all rich and don't need the money."

"Not exactly," said Sara. "Yes, they're all quite well-off, but I think it's more that they've made calculated decisions to make their money in the ways they know best. As I said, it wouldn't work for everybody. Someone else trying it could wind up very disappointed, and very broke, in retirement. This particular group has specific strengths that most people don't have. They took considerable risks to get where they are. It's not a foolproof plan, but it can pay off if you work hard and pick the right money-making idea.

"They all exemplify the old saw: 'Place your faith in the busy person, not the idler. If you want something done, find a busy person.'

"Oh yeah, I should forewarn you about 'The Game,'" she said.

"What game?" I asked. I secretly dreaded that someone would whip out cribbage or Scrabble boards.

"The game of life."

"What?"

"Never mind, it'll be explained. We get together every couple of months and usually someone gets around to playing The Game. There are no rules. You'll have no trouble getting the hang of it. It sure beats sitting around playing crib!"

Amen, I thought.

* * *

Gordon steered the jetboat into a floating aluminum dock where a man stood smiling, waiting to greet us—Doug Martini.

"Hellooo," he shouted before the boat even touched the dock. "Good ta see ya guys!" His accent sounded slightly southeastern U.S.

He ushered us up broad steps that swept from the beach to the cabin. On a very spacious deck sat five people all laughing and talking. Smoke fumed from a corner barbecue where a roasting chicken tantalizingly sizzled and spat.

I was introduced all around and patted Sheba, the dog.

The time before supper passed quickly. I was made to feel very welcome. I singled out Russ Waters to ask about the retirement village he was developing.

He explained he had picked up a piece of lake property, the site of a defunct sawmill, near Nelson during the 1980s recession. The strategic location of the 20-acre parcel, one mile east of the city, appealed to him. Initially he hadn't been sure what to do with it. He did know lakefront property would be increasingly difficult to come by. Besides, the selling price had been too good to pass up.

He held the property for a few years. Gradually an idea began to gel, helped by people on vacation who were visiting Nelson and looking seriously at property at the same time. They told Russ they hoped to retire there eventually.

Then Russ met Gordon and Sara and saw how The Last Resort worked. Voilà—the village concept and his piece of property seemed to mesh perfectly. After two years of planning, Russ announced that his development company was close to turning the first sod.

I was curious to know how his village would compare to The Last Resort.

"Oh, it'll be much more urban. The units will be condo style. Only about half the 140-unit development will be set aside for seniors, the other half for sale to the general public. The grounds will also be much more manicured than what you see at Gordon and Sara's; they have a real cabin feel out there that wouldn't work as well on this site. We don't have many trees, for example. And, in addition to the condos, we've attracted a hotel chain, some retail stores, and a full-service marina.

"When we're done there will be several hundred people and a pretty good range of services right on site, even transportation to the shopping mall and downtown, thanks to the extension of a lakefront trolley system we've almost sewn up."

"Sounds great!"

"Yes, it's a big move for Nelson. We've always been kind of stodgy here. Development and business actually flooded *out* in the eighties and the recession. Now small communities like Nelson, ones near the U.S. border with good weather, are really attracting a lot of interest from people right across the country. I think we're going to see quite a dramatic population spurt over the next decade. We want to be positioned to take advantage of that.

"So the image of a sleepy, out-of-the-way small city that prevented growth for so long is becoming one of our greatest strengths now."

I wondered how many other people recognized this quiet movement and, if it turned out to be accurate, when should a person make the move to avoid being caught on the wrong end of the inevitable price run-ups?

Supper was sumptuous. We wolfed down the chicken and a variety of green, potato, and pasta salads.

THE GAME

After the meal Doug and Sheena invited everyone back down to the beach where we arranged ourselves in comfortable chairs around a large metal fire pit. Doug lit some logs and asked, "So, who wants to play The Game?"

A round of yeas went around, except from me. Sheena noticed my silence.

"You can play. No problem, Richard."

"Okay. What do I have to do?"

"Think," contributed Russ Waters.

"Uh oh, that might cause a problem," quipped Gordon.

"Gordon! The game really isn't a game at all," Sara explained. "It's just brainstorming about life, so we call it the 'game of life.'"

"Sometimes there's more storm than brain," added Cosmo.

"Basically, we get together every couple of months. It's everyone's responsibility to come with one unusual idea or observation about where the world is going or something they want to do that is unusual. To make it relevant to us, the ideas have to concern something in which we could get involved if we wished and, given that this is a group of entrepreneurs, the ideas usually revolve around some new business concept. The only requirement is originality of thought."

"Sometimes it gets really original! One observation I've made," said Cosmo, "is that there is an inverse relationship between the quantity of wine and the quality of ideas. Speaking of inverse, would you mind inverting that bottle over my glass, Doug?"

"I should also add," Sara resumed, "that we usually have a theme and, in honor of your visit, the theme tonight is future world. It's not as serious as it sounds. The main idea is to have fun. It's also a good way to learn new things from other people— keeps our old brains working."

"Okay, I'm in," I said. Maybe Cosmo's idea about the wine would help.

Doug invited Gerard and Larissa to start.

"Well, our idea concerns the feasibility of setting up a national organization for the elderly. We know one exists already, the Canadian Association of Retired Persons, but from discussions we've been having with elderly clients it's apparent the potential for bringing people in this age group together hasn't even been scratched.

"So, we think sometime over the next decade, as the boomers really start to age, there's a ripe seed here ready to be planted. What do you guys think?"

"CARP for short," said Cosmo. "Is that like the fish or the whining old crone?"

"Neither," said Larissa.

"Well, I think the first thing you need is a better name. Who wants to belong to a CARP?" said Cosmo.

"What do you suggest, then?" said Larissa.

Cosmo thought for only a moment. "How about Seniors' League of Pensioners?"

I could see everyone doing the mental translation.

"That's SLOP, Cosmo!" said Sheena.

"SLOP, indeed," said Cosmo, "what a way to refer to my idea! Okay, maybe you're right. How about National Union of Retired People?"

"That's NURP," said Sara. "Even if it's nothing rude, it sounds bad."

"Boy, you guys are tough to please," said Cosmo. "I have one more. If you don't like this one I'm taking my wine and going home. How about Benevolent Union of Retired People?"

He rose and bowed amid the spontaneous laughter.

"Wait! I have one that might work," I volunteered.

"Okay," said Larissa, "you haven't been around Cosmo too much yet, have you?"

SEAL–C: Retirement Alliance
"Well, I admit I lack his wit. How about Senior Alliance of Canada. The acronym would be SEAL–C—sounds official."

"Good choice," said Russ. "Let's use SEAL-C as the discussion point."

"Okay, what would SEAL–C do?" asked Doug.

"Anything that retired people need it to do," Russ answered.

For example:

- Publish a monthly newsletter or magazine.
- Supply travel information.
- Arrange travel packages.
- Pass on merchandise discounts through the Association's bulk buying.
- Inform members about various health products.
- Provide financial advice.
- Develop insurance programs for seniors' health care, homes, autos, travel, and the like.

"The list could go on," he said. "There are lots of things this kind of organization could offer. The revenue potential would be huge. Just think of millions of Canadians all paying an annual membership fee plus extra fees for specific services."

"Good idea," said Doug, acting as unofficial chair for the game. "Let's hang that one on a hook and get back to it later to see if anyone here would actually consider taking on such a challenge. It could be a natural for Gerard and Larissa's business."

"Now that's a really good idea," said Gerard. "We promise we'll give you guys free memberships for a year if we do it."

"Big heart," said Gordon. "Don't forget, if you don't sweeten the pot for us we can always compete with you as SLOP or BURP."

"Okay, any other ideas?" asked Gordon. "How about you guys, Larissa?"

"We have one that might be good for someone with a piece of land."

"Okay," said Russ, "what is it?"

"An RV park for retired people who love to travel. They have them in the States, but the idea doesn't seem to have caught on much in Canada. Gerard and I read an article the other day about a couple in Arizona who are cleaning up running such a park.

They've taken the concept a step further by acting as a rental agency for those who want to get some money back from their RVs for the months they don't use them. They keep a list of rentals, maintain them while they're being rented, and take a percentage of rental fees. A few hassles if you get breakdowns, but still a nice business with very little outlay of cash themselves."

Another one for the hook.

"What did you guys come up with, Gord?" asked Doug.

"Actually, our idea would work well with both the ones discussed so far. It would offer seniors' adventure treks here in the West Kootenay. SEAL–C could promote the business and people interested in taking them could stay at the RV park.

"The younger, healthier retirees we're going to be seeing in a few years are going to be looking for interesting holidays and this area offers a lot of variety with the lake and mountains nearby. You could offer hikes, kayaking, boating, helicopter tours, back country skiing, gentler nature walks—the sky's the limit."

"Hey, you guys are sharp tonight," said Doug. "All three ideas are worth more thought. What else is rambling around in our brains tonight?"

Cosmo raised his hand

"Okay, Cosmo, the stage is yours," said Doug. Everyone sat back expectantly.

"Don't worry, it's nothing strange," he said. "You've all heard of virtual reality, right? Well, I understand they're nearing completion on creating virtual reality equipment that's effective over long-distance communications lines." He paused.

"So far, so good," said Sara. "What's the other shoe?"

"Why are you always so suspicious of my ideas?" asked Cosmo, looking hurt.

"Years of experience," said Sara. She was smiling.

"Anyway, this equipment includes transmitting and receiving body suits that are covered with tactile sensors. Four suits, two on dummies and two on participants, and all equipped with full-body tactile sensors enable you to transmit touch via long distance." He paused again.

"Why do we want to touch anyone long distance?" asked Sheena.

"Surely you see the potential," said Cosmo. "I mean you can literally transmit the sensation of touch. You put one suit on yourself—a receptor suit—and you put a transmitting suit on a dummy in your home, same at the other end. Then you can do whatever you want with the dummy and the person with the receiver suit on the other end feels the sensations. It's a way to have safe sex in the privacy of your home and you don't have to even meet the other person."

"Oh, gross," exclaimed Barb. "I don't want someone I don't even know touching me over the phone line!"

Even though it was a pretty offbeat idea I could see that everyone was thinking about it privately.

"As much as I hate to admit it," said Doug, "Cosmo's probably onto something. I haven't thought through all the ramifications, but I don't think there's much doubt somebody's going to make a lot of money out of the idea. And it does bring new meaning to the telephone slogan 'reach out and touch someone.'"

Groans from everyone but Cosmo. He clapped heartily at Doug's interpretation.

Ideas continued to flow.

"Fuel cells that run on oxygen and hydrogen and that produce electricity, heat and water without any pollution." The cells are already a reality according to a recent report. The group discussed the possibilities in getting the cells into arid climates where they could provide air-conditioning and water, a scarce commodity, at the same time. Another big money-making concept for that innovative somebody who succeeds in matching the cells with eager buyers with obvious needs.

"Mini-computers shaped like books." Huge strides have been made putting data on CDs, and some companies are already promoting these discs as replacements for books. Researchers are close to getting the data from 10,000 books on one CD. While we didn't question this technology, those of us who had actually tried to read a book off a computer screen were unimpressed.

The group opined that reading a book for leisure is a relaxation activity that just doesn't feel right when seated in front of a screen. Thus the idea of shaping a computer like a book so the reader could sink back into that easy chair by the fireplace and enjoy having 10,000 books at his/her fingertips. Somebody will do it.

"Credit card companies offer points for air miles, products and services, so why not RRSP contributions? People using a specific card would get credits, redeemable for cash if deposited in a registered RRSP account." People of all ages, and young people in particular, using such cards would accumulate considerable "compounding" contributions in an RRSP just by making purchases they would make without such incentive anyway.

After The Game ended, I had time to talk with both Doug and Russ. Their words echoed what Sara had told me in the boat ride on the way to the cabin.

Doug didn't disagree with the traditional retirement savings approaches—he just thought he did better using his own knowledge.

"What do I know about mutual funds and stocks?" he asked. "Give me the books from some hotel and I can tell you within an hour if it's making money and, if not, why it isn't. I just believe in making money by doing what I do best."

Russ said exactly the same thing.

"I have money in an RRSP but the returns have been dismal. So, I decided to take the money I used to put in RRSPs and invest it in real estate. It's not always a fast way to make money, but at least I know what I'm getting into and have a much better idea about the risk/reward ratio."

Entrepreneurs and Taxable Incomes

Doug brought up another important point: "When you're in business, your taxable income isn't always great. We have plenty of assets but we don't take large salaries. This means we don't have the kind of taxable incomes that the government insists on for maximum RRSP contributions. We would have to pay ourselves $75,000 each to put away the maximum $13,500 annually.

"If we, and many other business people, had to inflate our taxable incomes just to be able to make the maximum RRSP contributions, we'd be forced to extract too much money from the business and could actually damage our long-term profitability—the direct link of income to retirement savings doesn't always work for entrepreneurs. We believe our financial futures are going to be determined by the value of our businesses at the time we retire, and I'm sure a lot of other people are in the same boat."

I hadn't thought of that.

The evening passed too quickly. Finally back at Gord amd Sara's Last Resort, I lay awake in bed marveling at the vitality of these people, all at, or nearing, their retirements. Their gatherings struck me as more interesting, more challenging, and more educational than my usual ones in the city. Another lesson to take home.

We do not what we ought;
What we ought not, we do;
And lean upon the thought
That Chance will bring us through

— Matthew Arnold

CHAPTER 5

SLIPing into Your Future: Strategic Life & Investment Planning

Chapter Goal: To demonstrate tried and tested planning models for people who believe plans are better than no plans and that life should be approached systematically.

DAY 3, Morning

Another sunny morning. Fresh, cool air flooded through my open window. My head felt clear and my mind alert. I got up and looked down to the dock. There was Cosmo, punching and kicking the air. I looked at the clock on my bedside table. Only 5:30. I dressed and crept quietly out of the house. Might as well visit Cosmo. "So, what's the word this morning?" I asked, when I was close enough for him to hear.

Cosmo continued his smooth movements responding in a whisper without looking around, "The word is 'watch your step.'"

"Watch my step?" I asked.

"Yes, you're about to step in goose shit."

He laughed uproariously as I wiped my soiled shoe on the grass.

"I guess there's a lesson here, eh?"

"Not really," said Cosmo, "but since you seem to be in a receptive mood, how about, 'Just because you cannot successfully fight a thing, all need not be lost. Consider embracing it.'"

"Embrace goose shit?" I asked.

"Oh, okay, you don't like that one," Cosmo said. He pretended to meditate on this. "How about, 'There are ways to get your foot in the door and thus avoid the slam, to sweeten acerbity by asking the impatient and wrinkled housekeeper: "Is your mother home?"'"

"You had to mention 'foot,'" I said. "How do I get you to stop?"

"Well, I could answer, 'You move a man not by approaching him directly on a matter but by finding out who it is that has a rope tied to his foot.'"

"That's it, no more words of wisdom about feet. Is this your idea of a simple 'good morning?'"

"Oh, good morning, goose-hopper. So, you want some exercise before we start SLIPing?"

"I don't think I'd better do any fancy footing right now," I said, "or I'll be slipping, all right."

Still laughing, Cosmo gave me a collegial punch on the shoulder. I appreciated the comradery. My shoulder, on the other hand, ached for a few minutes.

As we walked back toward the cottage, he asked what I knew about strategic planning.

"Not a whole lot," I said. "It doesn't exactly sound like a trip to Disney World, though."

"No, I guess not," he said, "but it may do you a lot more good."

"Actually, seeing how you guys have spent so much time and given such careful thought to planning your lives, I feel like a bit of a flunk."

"Hey, goose-hopper, as my old friend Gibran says: 'To measure you by your smallest deed is to judge the power of the ocean by the frailty of its foam.' You seem like a bright young man and you have lots of time left before you head out to pasture. No sweat."

Cosmo and I found Gordon and Sara busy in the kitchen preparing coffee and cheese croissants.

"So," said Sara, "time for SLIPing, eh? I thought we'd have a working breakfast, so to speak. We can eat while Cosmo explains the process."

We settled ourselves around the table.

"First," Cosmo began, "a definition of Strategic Life & Investment Planning. Simply put, it provides

- an assessment of where you are now;
- a framework around which to define vision, values, and goals;
- a set of achievable actions; and
- a blueprint for implementing those actions so that they mesh with your goals.

"It usually helps if you read an explanation about the process before we get into details. Call it preplanning education."

He handed me some papers and I sat back to read.

If you don't know where you're going, any plan will do.

— Peter Drucker

STRATEGIC LIFE & INVESTMENT PLANNING (SLIP)

Strategic Life & Investment Planning poses straight questions and demands straight answers and then prompt action to correct deficiencies. It identifies individual aspirations and strengths, and isolates weaknesses and threats so you can deal with them constructively. It also means you can take advantage of opportunities.

SLIPing recognizes that turbulence is the norm in our lives. The only workable plan is one that allows for change without sacrificing vision or values. Your vision is written in stone, and it should not change unless you change. Your plans, however, are written in sand, so they can be adapted to match the changing world while you retain an unerring focus on your own vision.

Strategic Life & Investment Planning involves four stages:

- analysis,
- planning,
- implementation, and
- continuous monitoring and evaluation.

Conceptually, these stages translate into the following components:

1. Develop your vision of the future—dream a little but recognize barriers, too.
2. Establish your life and investment values.
3. Assess the internal environment—strengths, weaknesses, opportunities, and threats (SWOT).
4. Assess the external environment: opportunities and threats, economic, social, and technological forces and trends.
5. Formulate strategic directions and operations plans to manage issues and events.
6. Integrate an ongoing system of evaluation to determine whether your actions are in sync with what you're trying to do and where you're trying to go.

Developing Your Vision

If asked, many people will claim they know why they are doing what they are doing and that they know where they're going with their lives and their investments. Often, though, closer examination reveals very vague connections between the present and the future and actions and results. Why? There are two common reasons:

1. It is more reassuring to tell ourselves that everything is under control—questioning our current courses of action can cause anxiety.
2. It takes some knowledge and energy to evaluate realistically whether our actions are sound enough to take us successfully to that preferred "future," whatever it may be.

Without vision we spin our wheels in frustration and spread our resources too thinly.

I cannot overemphasize the importance of having a *stated* vision. Think of your vision as an optical lens. Place the lens (your vision) in front of your intentions and actions and gauge whether everything shows "clearly in focus." By holding your intentions and actions up to the vision "lens," you can check that the things in your control "fit" with your stated vision for life and retirement planning. If they "fit" together, you can pursue your course of action in some comfort. If there is no "fit," you should reconsider the wisdom of expending your energies or resources on that course of action.

Establishing Your Values

Everyone has values, but few people consciously apply their personal philosophies and values to their finance and retirement plans. Values require very careful thought. They must be something you can live by. The individual must believe in them, of course. Ideally, if you are part of a couple, both of you should agree on your priorities together.

Having defined values provides another "clarity lens" or check so you do not find you must sacrifice or compromise your philosophy about what is "right" in life now, and at retirement. Values provide your constant "measuring stick."

For example, if you are a committed environmentalist, you probably want to avoid activities in your life or in your financial matters, that offend your beliefs about preserving the physical world.

If you value honesty, integrity, and service to others, everything you do now, and in the future, should be in keeping with those concepts.

Environmental Scanning and SWOT Analysis

Environmental scanning and SWOT (Strengths, Weaknesses, Opportunities, and Threats) help establish and keep your investment plan on track.

These are forces that shape you and your life in infinite complex ways. You must understand, and confront, these same forces to achieve your own goals.

Environmental scanning tends to look at "external" forces and events, and SWOT analysis at "internal" ones. For example, environmental scanning will examine:

- family;
- place of work;
- friends and associates;
- the economies: local, regional, provincial, federal, global;
- technologies; and
- sociological factors that will affect your life and planning (such as demographics, community composition).

After you've completed a list, evaluate how these groups, people, and factors influence you and how they are likely to influence your intended actions. Take advantage of the positive influences and create strategies and possible approaches to help you cope best with the negatives.

SWOT analysis evaluates your personal strengths and weaknesses and the opportunities and threats that may affect your future activities and objectives:

- health and genetic predisposition(s);
- education;
- hobbies and interests;
- talents and skills;
- recreational interests;
- socialization abilities and attitudes;
- personal financial position; and
- career.

Sometimes you cannot always design strategies to cope effectively with every factor or trend identified in your own environmental scans and SWOT analyses. Expect to expend a "best effort" to minimize your chances of being blind-sided by something you could have foreseen and for which you might have developed a strategy.

Strategic Directions

Strategic directions are the specific goals you would like to accomplish to achieve your vision. Strategic directions are action-oriented objectives. Limit these to half a dozen at most, or you'll find the process too unwieldy.

Specific Life and Investment Plans

This is where the rubber hits the road. With your vision, values, and strategic directions clear in your mind and in place, you can decide how best to do the "work." Specific Life & Investment Plans are just that—specific. They detail precisely what you have to do to achieve your strategic directions, and they demonstrate a philosophical consistency between strategic directions, vision, and values.

Now, you face only one more stage.

Evaluation

Having a plan you ignore is little better than no plan at all. Check periodically that you are still on target, make any necessary adjustments, and give yourself reasons to celebrate your successes. Take pride in your SLIP; it represents invaluable information and strategies:

1. where you are now,
2. who you are and who you want to be,
3. what you are going to do and why you are going to do it,
4. when you will have it done, and
5. how you'll know when you have it done.

After I'd read the few pages, Cosmo asked if I thought I understood the concepts. I said I thought so.

"Well," he said, "we'll find out, because now we're going to ask you to put words to two of these planning components—vision and values.

DEVELOPING A VISION

"To develop a vision, pose some macro questions to yourself. For example:

- What is your preferred life in the years leading up to retirement and your preferred life after retirement?
- Where do you and your spouse want to be, and what do you want to be doing 20 or 30 years from now?
- If you could have three wishes for your retirement, what would they be?

"Think for a few minutes and write down your answers." In about 10 minutes I had jotted down the following:

Preferred Life Leading Up to Retirement

- Doing things we enjoy, including work and recreation.
- Not getting into a rut where time just seems to pass with few memorable or enjoyable things happening.
- Having more fun.

Preferred Life in Retirement

- Having our health and sufficient fiscal resources to do what we want.
- Retaining a zest for life and learning, doing new things, being creative.
- Escaping Canadian winters.
- Associating with interesting people.

Where Do We Want to Be and
What Do We Want to Be Doing in 20 to 30 Years?

- In a cottage on a lake from spring until fall while in Canada.
- Some place sunny and warm and interesting from winter until spring.
- Having fun and doing interesting, challenging, and creative things.

Three Wishes for Retirement

- Health, wealth, and happiness.

Establishing Values

I reflected hard on this and then wrote:

- respecting myself and my wife
- respecting the needs/wants and opinions of others
- honesty
- reciprocity
- willingness to help others less fortunate
- helping preserve the planet and respecting the rights of all that is on it—living and non-living
- maintaining an attitude that fosters continuous learning
- building wealth but not at the expense of others or the planet

*   *   *

When I was satisfied I had covered all the major ingredients, I announced I was finished. Cosmo took my sheets and read my points out loud while Gordon and Sara made notes. After he was finished they all looked at me.

"What?" I asked.

They all burst into laughter.

"Nothing," said Cosmo. "It's just always interesting to see what people come up with. You're a greedy capitalist with a conscience."

"I'm a what?" I wasn't quite sure what to make of that.

"Just kidding," said Cosmo. "Actually, it's great when we work with people who manage to mix a desire for wealth with a concern for others and the planet. They needn't be contrary goals. So, you've started your SLIP. How does it feel?"

"Not bad," I said. "It's interesting to put things I usually intellectualize into words on paper. I've never made a list like this, and I guess it does say a lot about who and what a person is."

"Yes, it does," said Cosmo, "and, just as important, you can now start thinking about strategic directions in a more meaningful and personal way. Without self-examination about where your heart and head reside, strategic directions would miss their mark, and specific life plans made without vision and values would lack soul and be impossible to follow.

"Happiness and fun seem to play important roles in your vision for the future. Do you know research has been done on what makes people happy? The important thing is that it isn't difficult to identify the common denominators in what it takes to make people happy."

What It Takes to Make Us Happy

"For example, people usually identify the following as contributing most meaningfully to their sense of happiness and contentment:

- Having a meaning and purpose in life
- Making a difference to others
- Having satisfying social relationships (conversations with others)
- Belonging to a group or community
- Being appreciated by other people
- Having family and friends
- Enjoying aesthetic pursuits and exercising your creativity
- Participating in meaningful work
- Feeling needed
- Enjoying health and vigor
- Pursuing adventure, novelty, challenge—to grow
- Exhibiting competence at home and on the job
- Feeling hopeful and optimistic about the future.

"Makes sense," I said. "I don't disagree with any of that. So, what's next?"

"Well, it also makes sense, does it not, to check your vision and values to see if your life is in sync? When, or if, you answer 'no,' to a question about yourself, you know you've identified something worth thinking about. Let's examine what you said.

"For this stage of your life, and for the years leading up to retirement, am I paraphrasing you accurately if I say you want to enjoy work and recreation, avoid getting into a rut, make more meaningful memories, and have more fun?"

"Yes," I said, "if we could do all that, I think we would have accomplished something pretty significant."

"You know the difference between a rut and a grave, don't you?" asked Cosmo, his eyes twinkling.

"Not really." I braced myself.

"Depth," he said, laughing.

"Oh great," I said, "now you're comparing my life to death. Is that supposed to make me feel better? I hope you guys aren't charging for this little seminar."

"Touchy, isn't he?" Cosmo asked Gordon and Sara.

"Only when you tell him the truth," said Gordon with a shrug.

I appealed to Sara. "Can't you control these guys?"

She laughed too. "I have some luck with Gordon, but Cosmo's permanently out of control and there's not much anyone can do."

"Okay," I said, "I gather I'm supposed to stay open to *constructive* criticism and I have to admit my ideals about life and living often seem to go awry in my day-to-day, but that pretty much mirrors everybody, I suspect. Changing sounds good, but it can't be easy."

"No, it's not easy," said Cosmo, "but you can do it if you develop a new mindset."

"What mindset?" I asked.

The Most Important Lesson of All

"Well, specifically to get yourself a new mindset that brings you more happiness, a person usually finds it necessary to force shifts in the ones that currently drive his or her attitudes and life. The shifts you want to strive for, of course, are the ones that lead to your personal version of what makes you happy. As with most things in life, you do have to work at this. To help people conceptualize what they need to do, I've developed a two-phase structure and process that I call "pattern recognition" and "deliberate joy manipulation." Any guesses about what these phases might entail?" he asked.

"Sure," I responded quickly, "sounds like you want me to recognize patterns and deliberately manipulate joy. Does she usually approve of this?"

"How very witty of you. Have you always been such a penetrating student?"

"Okay, so I took the easy way out. I gather you're going to explain them to me, anyway."

"I'd better!" he said. "But I want to suspend humor for a moment to emphasize that this is probably the most important stuff you're going to learn in your time here. Getting together a fat retirement fund is pointless if you have no ideas about how to enjoy it.

"So, with that bit of seriousness out of the way, let me ask you a question. 'What did you do last week that was particularly memorable and enjoyable?'"

I thought for a moment.

"I really can't think of anything out of the ordinary." I felt somewhat embarrassed.

"Right, then what did you do over the past month that you found particularly memorable or enjoyable?"

I thought again.

"God, if I answer 'nothing' again, you guys are going to think I lead a dull life! In truth, though, I really can't think of anything that was all that memorable or enjoyable."

"Tell us the last time you do remember doing something both memorable and enjoyable."

"That's better," I answered eagerly. "We had good times last summer sailing for a week with friends in the Gulf Islands."

"And the time before that?" he asked.

"Well, I guess our last annual vacation when we went to Hawaii, snorkeled, ate great food, read some good books, that kind of stuff."

"So, if I understand you correctly, you've had two memorable and joyful experiences over the past two years?"

"No, I've had more fun than that," I said defensively. "I just can't remember them all at the moment."

"Don't worry about it," he replied. "Actually, most people answer these questions pretty much the same way you did—that is, there are usually one, two, or three really memorable and joyful events over the course of a year. Hundreds of millions of people believe this is the way life plays out.

"Let me ask you now, though, how would you like to have a joyful experience not only once or twice a year, but every month, every week, maybe even every day?"

"Does it involve mind-altering drugs?" I asked in disbelief.

"No, it does not. It involves pattern recognition and deliberate joy manipulation."

"Back to those," I said.

"Yes, five words that can easily change your life. Now I'm going to tell you how. Do you recognize a pattern in your most memorable and enjoyable times?"

I thought. "Sure, usually when we're on vacation, and sometimes we do memorable things on long holiday weekends."

"Right," he said. "Is there any reason you restrict your good times to holidays and long weekends?"

"We don't restrict having fun to those times," I said. "Those are just the times we plan special things."

"Precisely," he said with a grin. He looked quite proud of himself. "How'd I do?"

"Very well, goose-hopper. You've recognized your happiness pattern and also your version of deliberate joy manipulation."

"I have?"

"Is he always this thick?" Cosmo asked Gordon and Sara.

"Be patient with him, master," Sara put in. "This having-fun stuff is a whole new world to most baby gloomers."

"You're right," clucked Cosmo. "Young people these days. You do get what I'm talking about?" he asked me seriously.

"Yes, I get it," I said. "You're saying that we only seem to have good times when we *plan* to have good times, and herein lies my pattern and my deliberate joy manipulation."

"All you need to do is engrain that pattern recognition and learn to plan more memorable and joyful events on a daily, weekly, and monthly basis. Doing this is easier with your annual vacation because people usually plan special things then, anyway. But you aim to use a similar process to boost your joyful times to dozens of events over the course of the year instead of just two or three!"

"I think I feel a plan coming on," I said, placing my hand to my forehead.

"You certainly do," said Cosmo. "And a plan that leads to fun can't be all that painful, can it?

"I sure hope not!"

"What about your daily life? What could you do every day that would add real joy and a sense of expectation to your day? I should add that they shouldn't be things that cost a lot of money or that take too much time. Trying to fit expensive or time-consuming joy into busy lives rarely works since people run out of money, time, and energy."

"Oh sure," I complained. "Now you want me to be joyful, but cheap and quick about it!"

"You got it!" he said.

Deliberate Daily Joy

"Well, two things I always say I'm going to do, but seldom get around to, are reading for enjoyment and using the hot tub we got a few months ago to relax at the end of the day."

"Why *don't* you do these things?" he asked.

I snorted. "I guess you won't be surprised if I tell you we run out of time and energy."

"That sounds more like excuses than reality. Surely you could fit in a half hour in the morning and a half hour at night in bed to read for enjoyment. Why don't you move your supper hour back a half hour, pop open the lid of the hot tub and jump in with Lorraine and a couple of glasses of wine every night as soon as she gets home from work? That's one and a half hours in your day that I'm sure you could 'budget.' If you did only this, it would become your dollop of daily enjoyment. They aren't big things, but they could become part of an enjoyable routine that would add to your new knowledge, and give you both some relaxation and discussion time together. What do you think?"

"I think you guys are all too clever for your own good, sitting here in lotusland by the lake thinking up ways other people can enjoy themselves!"

"Well, actually, we find ways to enjoy ourselves while we're doing it, so we're not entirely selfless," he said. "In fact, a hot tub sounds pretty good about now. But, it will have to wait a little while longer."

Deliberate Weekly Joy

"So, now you've added two little joys to your daily life. How about something you could do every week?"

"Okay." I considered.

"How about skiing at least once a week in winter, or going out for a nice dinner every Friday night, or getting out on the water at least once a week when the weather's nice?"

"Sounds good," he said, "but most people might have trouble with the expense of skiing and eating out every week."

"Well, if money's tight we could do pizza and a movie every Friday or Saturday or go cross-country skiing in winter and camping in summer."

"Great!" said Cosmo. "Plan joyful activities that are attainable. The really important thing is not to let your good intentions lapse into nonaction.

"You're already planning deliberate joy annually for your vacations, so it just leaves a monthly plan to add to what you've worked up for your daily and weekly joy, and you'll be the most joyful guy on your block."

"Are you telling me it's that easy?"

"No, I'm not, and it's not," said Cosmo, looking a little impatient. "In fact, most people have trouble changing their existing life patterns for ones that offer more consistent, planned joy. For this reason I've developed worksheets that enable anyone interested in the idea to put things down on paper. This lets most people visualize 'what could be.' Getting it in writing makes some people feel more committed to carrying it out. Plus, they've got something to refer to when they want to check their own progress or direction. Give me a minute, and I'll get the materials."

He returned in a few minutes with a package of papers.

"Here, read this. Gordon and Sara have already been through this so we'll just wait while you go through it, too."

I read, again.

IMPROVING YOUR LIFE

Our parents and grandparents lived in a duty culture, duty to family, work, the church, etc. Today, however, we live in a sensate culture. "I'll do it if it feels good.

— Dr. Gary Phillips

Life improvement uses self-analysis to stimulate behavioral change. There are six stages:

1. Analyzing yourself and reflecting
2. Mentally creating a new, better condition
3. Committing yourself to making a change
4. Implementing the change
5. Evaluating yourself
6. Rewarding yourself

You begin a planned, purposeful improvement in your life by establishing a clear mental picture of what the improved state of your life would "look" like. First, you need the vision. Having that is a tremendous step forward.

To change, you need to understand what gives you joy and learn to recognize patterns you would like to repeat. Joy occurs in almost everyone's life from time to time. You can ensure it occurs much more frequently if you learn how to orchestrate positive events and to plan ways to improve your professional and personal activities.

The kinds of involvements that typically bring us "joy" include new learning, new achievements, worthwhile endeavors, struggle, and even failure, when we can see it as evidence of extension and challenge.

Here's a how-to plan:

TOWARD LIFE IMPROVEMENT

Time required: 10 minutes a day

1. Review yesterday. Recall one thing that made you happy—a professional or personal source of pride: new knowledge gained, new friend made, act of kindness performed, etc.
2. Analyze what made you happy. Did you do anything to contribute to that happiness? Was it part of a planned activity? Who else was involved? Was it something they planned? In looking at your past, are there common threads in the types of activities that make you happiest or most joyful?
3. Did you learn something new yesterday—valuable information, improved skills, altered beliefs, mindsets, or attitudes as a result of your experiences and relationships?
4. Did you fail at anything yesterday? Failure can lead to analysis, action, and improvement. People derive considerable self-gratification from learning to overcome obstacles. Life can be boring if you never stretch yourself beyond your own areas of competence. Plan to do something beyond your capabilities, analyze why you can't do it, correct deficiencies, succeed, pick a new area of deficiency. Continue cycle.

Happiness checklist: family; work, play, self, finances, physical fitness, social life, other?

Try New Learning Styles

"To borrow an old phrase," said Cosmo, "the only thing people have in common is that they are different. In this same vein, everyone has individual 'preferred' learning styles. This doesn't mean people *should* have only one or two styles—it's just that most of us don't even think about developing additional ones. Strange, isn't it, that we don't spend much time thinking about the *way* we think?

"At any rate, if you're going to deliberately try to extract more joy from life, it's important that we all expand our minds to become lateral thinkers more than linear thinkers."

"Are we into football now?" I asked.

"Sort of," said Cosmo. "Same concept regarding a lateral. I'm sure from the workplace, and life, you've seen how people respond to a situation in the most direct line—the path of least resistance—to solve a problem or deal with a situation?"

"Sure, getting something dealt with as quickly as possible seems most efficient," I said.

"Sometimes it is," said Cosmo, "but *always* being linear means people miss out on some novel, and sometimes truly elegant, solutions. I'm sure you've had occasions when you thought you had an easy answer to something and then someone else came up with a different approach and you thought, 'Why didn't I think of that?'

"Well, that's usually a sign of someone engaging in lateral thinking. Try to consciously view every situation from the sides, bottom, top, and back, as well as from the front. You'll often be surprised at how much more creative your solutions will be when you deliberately force a change in perspective."

"Give me an example." I wasn't quite sure how I was supposed to envision every situation having sides, bottoms, tops, and backs.

"Okay, that's easy," he said. "Think about The Last Resort. Just a few years back, retired people faced fewer choices about what to do for accommodation when they quit work. Most stayed in homes that were often too large or too much trouble to maintain, or in which they had far too much capital tied up. Many of these people presumed that the only other option was to buy a small, cramped apartment or move into an old folks' home—and these prospects aren't necessarily attractive.

"Well, there must have been a lateral thinker involved at some stage who thought, 'These traditional housing solutions for retired people aren't good enough. What do people really want and how could it be achieved?' That's the beginning of a lateral thinking plan and I'm sure it's how retirement villages came about. The moral of this story is: don't always be satisfied with the first, easiest solution—there's often a much better one lurking in your head if you take the trouble and energy to turn ideas over and over.

"So, do you think you can employ lateral thinking now, and *know* you're employing it?"

"Yeah, I think so," I said, "this whole week has been one huge lateral. I don't think I'll ever be the same."

"Sounds like an improvement," shot in Gordon.

"Be nice," said Cosmo. "Okay, now that we've discussed shifting your thinking orientation, let's look at the ways most people learn. I can summarize them quickly: 1) reading; 2) watching; and 3) listening. Do any of these describe how you learn?"

"I remember things best if I can read about them and then have the new knowledge reinforced visually somehow. I don't tend to learn well just by listening."

"You're not alone there," said Cosmo. "Very few people are audio learners. In fact, none of the three learning modes I mentioned is particularly effective if you really want to retain information. Do you know why?"

"I think you're going to tell me."

"You got it. Because most of the time they don't get learners *involved*. You must experience to learn. There are many ways of learning something but there is one rule that applies to every learning technique: *without emotion there is no learning.*

"Or, if you want something to help you remember, I use one of Gordon's acronyms—BIIQ, which stands for Benefit, Interest, and Impact Quotient. With BIIQ he tries to demonstrate that if the receivers of any communication see no benefit to it, aren't interested, or fail to see how it will affect them, the information goes right through the old noggin. So, no BIIQ—no stick.

"Do you buy all of this?"

"Sure, it makes sense. We certainly remember things that are relevant to us and things that get us charged up.

"Great. Now the trick is to think about new ways of getting joy into your life and figuring out ways to take the new strategies from ideas to action. Here's a worksheet to help organize your thoughts."

A YEAR IN YOUR LIFE: PLANNING CHANGES

1. Reflection

Where you would like to be in one year's time? What new knowledge or skills would you like to have? How would you like to improve yourself in your relationships? At work? Write down your ideal vision of yourself one year from today.

2. Action Plans

What specific actions must you take to work toward each of the improvements you want to achieve over the coming year? For example:

One year from today, I will have gained enough expertise and developed skills to start a new business in an area about which I feel passionate.

One year from today, I will have improved my attitudes to become a more caring spouse, a better parent, a better colleague, etc.

---

3. Implement Your Action Plans

Set a firm timetable to act on your goals and follow it!

4. Strengths and Weaknesses

List the strengths and weaknesses you will have to overcome to complete your goals successfully. Anticipate and plan ways to conquer problems, for example: plot how to maintain your focus, how to make time to attain the new skills you need, and so on.

5. Evaluate

People can play tricks on themselves. They can set themselves goals that are too easy or too difficult to measure. You have to decide what constitutes acceptable effort and achievement for the goals you set yourself.

6. Reward Yourself

Improving your life, skills, and knowledge deserves celebration and reward. Make your reward to yourself reflect the degree of effort and time you've devoted to your success. For example, earning a master's degree or paying off the mortgage might warrant a trip to Hawaii, while learning better time management skills might warrant a ski weekend.

I looked up from my reading again. "Well, that certainly provides some structure for planning achievements."

"Yes, doesn't it?" said Cosmo. "At this stage, you should be prepared to develop strategic directions that outline what you want to do and then the Specific Life & Investment Plans of what you have to do to achieve them."

"Okay," I said, "let's do it."

"Eager student!" said Cosmo, pleased.

"Actually, I'm feeling better about this. Having a structure does make it seem doable."

"It *is* doable, for anyone who wants to do it. Let's tackle strategic directions that flow logically from your vision."

DEVELOPING STRATEGIC DIRECTIONS

"To make this comprehensible," said Cosmo, "we'll restate your vision for your lifestyle leading up to retirement:

- Doing things we enjoy, including work and recreation.
- Not getting into a rut where time just seems to pass with few memorable or enjoyable things happening.
- Having more fun.

"Without getting specific about the actual 'how's,' what do you think you have to do in a macro sense to move in the right directions?"

"In truth," I said, "they all seem quite interconnected. And my perceptions will differ a bit from Lorraine's."

"That's to be expected. What do you mean?"

"Well, we're always talking about putting more enjoyment in our lives. I guess I'd have to break it down into two parts: work and recreation.

"I enjoy my work for the most part—I get to write and research and meet interesting people. But Lorraine doesn't like her job. She spends 40-plus hours a week doing something she'd rather not be doing and that tends to color her perspective."

"So," said Cosmo, "it comes down to identifying directions for work and play. Only Lorraine can decide on how to make her work life more enjoyable, but if she wants to approach this logically, and from the point of view that it is an incredible sacrifice to spend a third of her life being miserable, she should make some kind of change."

"I know she agrees with that," I said. "It's just difficult to cut ties with a career that she's had for 25 years and for which she had to get a university degree. She's got 30 years invested in it and, to top it all off, she's really good at it."

"This is a difficult one," said Cosmo. "Many people find themselves locked into jobs they don't really like. You have to ask yourself whether the money, prestige, or security outweigh the downsides. Often, shifting your life into an area where a person is happier is worth the trouble. Usually what they think they're giving up doesn't seem so important after they're distanced from it for a while and much more content in the new endeavor.

"Maybe after you and she go through this process together and she sets a new vision and values for herself, her choice about precisely what to do will become easier.

"But since she's not here to participate, let's look at where your recreational lives seem to be lacking and try to identify where you'd rather they be. When you two are talking about preferred activities, what kinds of things come up?"

"That's easy," I said. "As people who seem to experience too many days without positive memorable or joyful events in them, I'd say our most memorable and joyful times come from several things:

- winter holidays to new, interesting places;
- spending as much of summer as possible on the boat and camping;
- skiing;

- getting together with friends and exploring new ideas about everything under the sun; and
- pursuing personal hobbies that we both enjoy."

"Those don't sound unreasonable," said Cosmo. "Why aren't you doing them all?"

"I don't know," I said. "We seem to get so caught up in the urgent that we forget the important. The days just go by. Some years we don't even take a sun or ski holiday because we're trying to save money for—guess what—our damn retirement and the other bills that always seem to come along."

Cosmo nodded. "You're not that unusual, there are millions of people who would relate a similar story, I'm sure. The tragedy is just that your aspirations aren't outlandish—it's just your resolve to do them that's in question."

"Yeah, right," I said, feeling a bit foolish.

"SLIPing isn't about recrimination," said Cosmo; "it's about designing achievable plans to get rid of the need for recrimination.

"We're getting to the good part now: you know what you'd like to do and why you're not doing it. Let's get an official strategic direction and action plan down on paper. Let me take a shot at writing the first one, then you change it to suit yourself, and you can do the rest."

He spent a few minutes with my "wants" and then said: "'**Strategic Direction #1:** Take an annual winter holiday to a new and interesting place.' How does that sound?"

"It sounds great," I said, "but saying it isn't the same as doing it."

"You're right," he said. "That's where the SLIPing of SLIPing comes into play."

"Pardon?"

"Your Specific Life & Investment Plans, another SLIP acronym. What kind of a plan could you put in place to achieve strategic direction #1?"

"Call the travel agent and book the flight would be one way to get committed," I said, only half serious.

"Actually, that's not bad," said Cosmo, "but there might be a way to approach it from the front instead of the back."

"What front, what back?" I asked.

"Well, just booking the flight would get a commitment, but the commitment might be less stressful if you take the financial aspects into account. You did say, after all, that the reason you don't always take a holiday is because of money diverted to other seemingly more pressing areas."

"Right."

"Okay, so what if when you get home and see if Lorraine's onside, you contact your bank and set up an automatic debit into a holiday account—say $200 every two weeks? That would add up to $5,200 for a holiday. Could your budget handle this and, if so, is the annual sum enough, or do you guys stay at the Hilton?"

"We could adjust to the automatic withdrawal," I said. "I know from past experience that people have a remarkable way of making a budget work when money is shunted off automatically. If it's in the checking account, you spend it. If it isn't, you get by and pretty soon cease to even think about it. And, yes, it would come close to being enough. We might have to come up with another thousand or two at the time of the holiday but, after all, we would spend money even if we stayed home and didn't take the holiday, so there would be some more money available from our usual monthly budget."

"Right," he said. "You now have Specific Life & Investment Plan #1."

"I do?" I asked.

"You do," he said.

> "'**Specific Life & Investment Plan #1:** Open a separate holiday bank account within two weeks and channel $200 into this account every two weeks. It will not be spent for anything else.'"

Intentions without action = an unfulfilled life.

"Have you got the concept?" he asked.

"I think so. I'll take a shot." I thought a moment and wrote:

> **Strategic Direction #2:**
> Plan daily and weekly events that are fun and memorable.
>
> **Specific Life & Investment Plan #2:**
> Use the life-improvement-plan concept to systematically develop and commit to learning and doing something new and interesting.

"Great," said Cosmo. "You may want to be even more specific about your specifics, too. For example, if you want to spend more time with interesting people to have your challenging discussions, you might consider starting a 'gourmet supper club' that gets together according to some sort of schedule—perhaps monthly. You could try new ethnic foods and set up something like we did at the Martinis' where you have a varied agenda to discuss economics, politics, philosophy, future world, or whatever.

"Getting a group together weekly might be pushing it, although some people do. It's even easier in retirement. But you could plan more personal experiences for yourselves daily or weekly. Exactly *what* will vary with each person, but the objective is to think about it seriously and get into the habit of doing it. It's like exercise—if you do it regularly it gets easier, and you start to miss it if you skip a day or a week."

"Speaking of health," I said, "one of my visions concerns having our health and sufficient fiscal resources to do what we want in retirement. I guess I could develop a strategic direction and specific action plan for that:

Strategic Direction #3:
Maintain our health now so we have a better chance of enjoying life in the future.

Specific Action & Investment Plan #3:
Join a gym and work out four times a week.

"And I guess part 3A could concern finances:

Specific Life & Investment Plan #3A:
Implement the Investment & Savings Plan outlined at The Last Resort.

"How am I doing?"

"Great! Those are both specific so you can easily evaluate whether or not you're deviating from the plan."

"I know Lorraine will have some visions about doing something for the environment. To be honest, I try to do my bit for recycling and not polluting, but it's kind of like paddling up Niagara Falls. She's really committed, though, and I have to admire her for it."

"Sounds like Lorraine's a lot like the little boy from Maine," said Cosmo.

"What little boy from Maine?"

"Tell her this story when you get home. I think she'll appreciate it. It's about making a difference:

In Maine they tell of an old man walking along the beach with his grandson. The boy picked up each starfish they passed and threw it back into the ocean. "If I left them here," said the boy, "they would dry up and die. I'm saving their lives."

The old man said, "But the beach goes on for miles and there are millions of starfish. What you're doing won't make any difference."

139

The boy looked at the starfish in his hand, threw it into the water, and answered, "It makes a difference to this one."

"Nice story," I said. "I'll try to do it justice."

"Well," said Cosmo, "if you think you have the SLIPing concept firmly in hand, I would suggest taking the rest of the visions back and completing the process with your wife. If you systematically go down the list of visions and match them with strategic directions and specific action plans, you should have all the important bases covered, including the one about being in a cottage by the lake when you retire.

"Who knows? Maybe we'll be neighbors someday."

You can't leap a wide gorge by taking small steps.

Investment plans are very unforgiving. They don't tolerate procrastination and they have no sympathy when ignored or deviated from. Their performance is dependent on planners who set goals in stone—movable goals are as dependable as sand.

CHAPTER 6

RRSPs: A Unique Short Course

Chapter Goal: To detail RRSP planning concepts and provide a range of lifestyle and saving scenarios.

DAY 3, Afternoon

We finished the SLIPing exercise by noon and moved out to the patio to enjoy a light, tasty lunch of herb soup and veggie sandwiches.

"How does your brain feel?" asked Sara.

"I think it's still there," I answered.

"Do you think it's receptive to more information?"

"Sure, as long as it's interesting information."

"We'd never dump boring information on you," she said. "Our job is either to show you a good time or scare the hell out of you to be sure you remember what we discuss!"

"If I get a vote, how about showing me a good time as opposed to the alternative?"

"Okay, I think we can do that. The topic this afternoon will be RRSPs, and I don't propose to cover the stuff you've probably already read. There are many good books on RRSPs, and there's little point in repeating them. I'll touch on the obvious 'do's,' then move to helpful material and scenarios.

"There's been a lot of publicity about RRSP planning in recent years. The ways to proceed are pretty clear-cut. Let's summarize the actions of

THE SMART RRSP PLANNER

1. You owe a debt to yourself.

"Most people arrange their finances something like the following: a) earn money; b) pay debts; and c) maybe save whatever's left over. To my way of thinking, 'c' is at the wrong end of the equation. It's been said before, and written about by several noted financial advisers, that more people would retire a lot happier and wealthier if they moved themselves to the top of the creditor heap. In other words, they owe it to themselves to pay themselves first for future needs.

"Specifically, we think that a given percentage of all income, somewhere in the 10-percent range, should be viewed as long-term personal debt, like a mortgage to yourself, whereby you make payments on the 15th and 30th of each month and the accumulating sum is left alone for retirement. There should be no fudging with this regular debt obligation. I recommend that you protect it with an automatic withdrawal from every paycheck.

"It's curious how people will make loan payments and mortgage payments every month for decades and never miss a single one. But once they put personal savings at the end of the money management process, it tends to assume a lower priority. People should tell themselves from age 20 that they owe themselves 10 percent of every net dollar earned and that this 10 percent is their first debt obligation. If they did, you and I wouldn't be talking like this now!"

2. Start as early in life as possible.

"Folks could retire wealthy if they simply started saving money at age 25 and contributed just a couple of thousand dollars a year until age 65. The nest egg would be worth much more than a million dollars if we average annual returns anywhere near 10 percent.

"However, the situation becomes much trickier for those who don't start saving for retirement until they're in their thirties. Many people don't get around to starting RRSPs until they're in their late forties. This apparently late start owes a lot to fiscal realities associated with raising a family and paying off a lifetime of debts and a mortgage.

"The good news is that even starting at these late ages doesn't mean a comfortable retirement is out of the question. We'll run some examples to show you how in a while."

3. Make the maximum contribution you're allowed.

"Making the maximum contribution is an obvious plus. It's also well known that you should make that contribution early in the calendar year so your funds compound for longer. It makes a big difference over a lifetime. Statistical projections prove that contributing your maximum RRSP allowance every January for the given year means you'll have an extra year of income in your RRSP by the time you retire!

"Making the maximum contribution also gives you the maximum tax benefit and puts the most money in a tax-sheltered haven."

4. Don't take silly risks but don't be overly conservative, either.

"Having 20 to 30 years to go to retirement means your retirement fund can weather several business cycles and the odd downturn won't kill you. For example, someone with $150,000 in an RRSP today who contributes an additional $10,000 per year and earns 5-percent interest in a safe bond or GIC will have $718,653 after 20 years.

"By contrast, someone with the same $150,000 making the same $10,000 contribution, but earning 10 percent per year, will have $1,571,880 in the RRSP in 20 years. You'll notice that the total from earning 10 percent is *more* than twice as much as earning 5 percent—$853,227 more to be exact. So you can see that being safe might be more comforting, but it won't work any miracles for your retirement.

"Now, 5 percent is probably low for an earnings projection, and 10 percent may be high, although the track record of the stock markets over the long term proves that such a gain, on average, is quite possible. The point is you have to be aware of the huge difference a few percentage points can make."

5. Take advantage of the $2,000 overcontribution limit.

"Although it is not tax-deductible, the funds the $2,000 helps compound in your RRSP do accumulate without tax. For a couple, a $4,000 investment now can buy two strip bonds worth about $2,000 each that will mature in the year 2023 for $40,000—a tax-sheltered gain of $36,000."

6. Risk outside, safe inside.

"If you have both RRSP and non-RRSP investments, there are very good reasons for keeping your safest investments in your RRSP. For example, keep strip bonds and such interest-bearing instruments inside an RRSP, but any stocks outside. Why?

"If you lose money in an RRSP, you aren't allowed to 'make it up.' By this I mean the government doesn't allow you to re-contribute funds that are lost. Conceivably, a person taking a risk in an RRSP could lose the entire fund—and then it's lost forever.

"If you lose money in an RRSP you can't write off the losses on your taxes.

"The capital gain on stocks held in a non-RRSP portfolio aren't taxed until you sell the stock; you must pay tax, however, on annual interest for strip bonds and other such instruments even though they may not mature for 30 years—you pay each year.

"If you need to borrow money for stocks outside an RRSP, you can write off the interest you pay on the loan to buy the stocks."

7. Protect your RRSP funds: buy securities outside the RRSP.

"The federal government lets you make contributions in kind to your RRSP. These contributions in kind can be stocks, for example, and buying them outside your RRSP and then transferring them into it can be a wise strategy. Why, you might ask?"

"Yes, why?"

"Because you can pay the brokerage fees outside your RRSP. To demonstrate, let's suppose you're going to put stocks in your RRSP because you don't have any non-RRSP investments. We'll also assume you want to make your maximum $13,500 annual contribution.

"So, you buy $13,500 worth of a stock outside your RRSP and pay 2.5-percent brokerage fees—that's $337.50. The next day you instruct your broker to transfer the stock into your RRSP. You get the benefit of the entire $13,500 credited. If you bought the stock inside your RRSP, the brokerage fees of $337.50 would be deducted from your RRSP; that's $337.50 less to compound for 30 years. At our standard 6-percent growth projection, that $337.50 would grow to almost $1,100 in 20 years. Follow a similar strategy for multiple stocks and you could easily end up with an extra $10,000 at retirement age.

"I should note, however, that there is one wrinkle the government throws at you. The transfer of the stocks into your RRSP is deemed to be a sale, so if you've realized a capital gain on the stocks, you'll have to pay tax on it in that tax year. But if you transfer the stocks in quickly—it usually takes about three days—the tax implications should be minimal."

8. Take advantage of past unused contribution room.

"In the 1996 federal budget, the government removed all time limits on using past contribution room in RRSPs. This means that people who don't have the money, or the discipline, to contribute their maximum allotments to their RRSPs, can make up the contributions for those years they were short at any time

in the future. This is a big improvement over the previous
restriction, which permitted people to make up contributions for
only the previous seven years.

"If this new rule stays in effect, it really helps procrastinators
and young people! Suppose, for example, that you're 30 years of
age, raising a family and haven't had the money to contribute to
an RRSP because you were buying a house in the city. Now,
suppose you decide to move from the city to a smaller town with
cheaper real estate. You sell your city house for $250,000 and
buy a comparable place in the smaller town for $150,000.

"The $100,000 surplus is tax-free because it's a gain on your
principal residence. The neat thing about this new rule, though,
is that you could take a good portion of that $100,000 and stick
it in your RRSP and claim deductions on your taxable income
for several years!

"For example, assuming you were earning about $45,000 a
year but contributed nothing to your RRSP for several years,
you could use the $100,000 to top up your 18 percent RRSP
allowance ($8,100) for every year you had missed in the past."

9. Having trouble saving? Read about the "Forgo Three Raises Plan."

"I know many people have difficulty putting away the amount
of money the government allows for RRSPs, and the usual argument goes something like: 'I can barely make ends meet now, so
how am I supposed to save $5,000 a year for my RRSP?' My
response is to ask these people how many raises they've received
in recent years. For example, if you were a federal government
employee from 1991 until 1996, you wouldn't have received a
single raise because the federal service froze its employees'
wages. Fortunately, Ottawa decided to remove the freeze in 1996
so there were small increases for these workers again.

"The interesting thing is that 99.9 percent of federal government workers managed to survive those five years even though

they received no raises during that period. Being frozen amounted to a real-wage decrease of about 10 percent when you calculate the effect inflation had on prices.

"Now, my premise is that, if they choose not to apply some savings discipline, most people will quickly get accustomed to spending whatever amount of money they make. If they don't get a raise, they simply adjust expectations so they survive; if they do get a raise they adjust their expectations and spend a bit more.

"What I suggest for people who have difficulty saving is that they forgo their next three salary increases by advising their bank to transfer every cent of those raises into an RRSP account. I would also counsel that they do the same with the tax rebate they get as a result of having made the RRSP contribution. If people would do this they could dramatically increase their RRSP savings and they wouldn't have to give up a cent of the money they now net. What they would give up is expecting that extra income. But if you look down the road a few years and ask yourself if passing up three raises is worth a comfortable retirement, I wouldn't be surprised if a lot of people said 'yes.'"

10. Apply for a tax-deduction waiver.

"It makes good fiscal sense to contribute your total RRSP allotment as early in each New Year as possible. There is also a little-known strategy for people who have trouble saving the money in advance or who are tempted to spend their tax rebates each spring instead of putting them back into their RRSPs.

"It's called a tax-deduction waiver. You get the waiver from Revenue Canada. This in turn notifies an employer to deduct less tax from an employee's paycheck because that person is making monthly RRSP contributions, which are, of course, tax-deductible. In essence, this plan allows you the value of immediately reduced taxes as long as you can prove you are making those RRSP contributions.

"If, for example, someone had RRSP room of $3,600, and she

149

was in the 50-percent tax range, she could apply to Revenue Canada to pay $1,800 less in taxes. After being notified by Ottawa about the waiver, her employer would leave $150 more on each month's net pay to her, which she would apply to making investments. She would do well to get an investment firm to buy a mutual fund in her name using the dollar-cost averaging approach.

"Most people would find it easier to ask an investment adviser for a waiver application—most brokerage houses have them—but you can do the procedure yourself. Just remember you must have proof that you are making those monthly RRSP contributions.

"I noticed," said Sara, "that your eyebrows rose when I mentioned dollar-cost averaging. Are you familiar with the term?"

"No."

"Well, it's a simple concept, really. All it requires is that you commit to investing a certain amount of money every month, or every quarter, to something like a mutual fund or stock purchase plan. Then you buy mutual-fund units or shares regularly and without fail. You buy both when prices are high and when they're low. When prices are low you get more units for your investment; when prices are high you get fewer. This means that, on average, over the long haul, your per unit costs will be lower because you're buying more during market dips than during market highs. Another bonus with this system is that you can stop worrying about market fluctuations, and you're in the market consistently. History and research prove that the gains you'll make will add up like clockwork."

11. Other saving strategies.

"Many people claim they simply can't save money for their retirement. I know in some cases people's finances are so finely stretched that they may not have any cash left over once their income is applied to their absolutely necessary expenditures. No question—people in this situation face a very difficult problem. And I don't have easy answers for them.

"But I also know there are other people who claim to be unable to save who really could. They just choose not to save. True, they may spend every cent of their incomes, but analysis of their cash flows demonstrates that their lifestyle choices are often what wipe out their savings potential, not necessities.

"For example, millions of Canadians still smoke. Now, I'm not going into a tirade against smoking—people make their own health choices. Yet consider how much money is spent on this habit and the wonders it could do in smokers' RRSPs. Let's look at two fictional smokers, both 40 years of age, one who burns a full package a day and the other who smokes only half a pack. We'll assume both have 25 years to go till retirement and that the full-pack-a-day person spends $5 a day and the half-pack-a-day person $2.50.

"The pack-a-day person will spend $5 x 365 days x 25 years = $45,625 over 25 years. The other person spends half that, or $22,813. Now, if that money were invested annually, to the tune of $1,825 and $913 respectively, for each year over those 25 years, we're talking hundreds of thousands of dollars! People spending almost $200 a month on cigarettes who have no money left over are seeing more than tobacco go up in smoke.

"As we've said before, saving for retirement, or saving for anything for that matter, is often a matter of the choices people make. I have a lot of sympathy for young people with low incomes who can barely keep roofs over their heads and groceries in the cupboard, but a lot of other people could trim in any number of areas to sock away that $200 a month toward a comfortable retirement.

"Besides making your own wine or cutting cigarettes down or out, people should really examine other expenditures, too, before they plead poverty. I can give several simple examples of saving without really reducing the quality of your life. Do all of them and you can be thousands of dollars ahead each year:

- drive a less expensive vehicle and cut your car and insurance payments in half;
- beer drinkers—drink one less per day, bank the $2 saved;
- eat out less frequently;
- buy fewer fashionable clothes;
- cut your grocery bill—get your protein quotient by substituting bean dishes for meat dishes 10 times a month;
- make your house more energy-efficient and bank the savings;
- get one of those piggy banks you can't open to see what's inside. Then, *every* day, stick those pesky loonies and twoonies in it that you find in your pocket or purse—for most people, this can add up to a $1,000 a year;
- avoid those lottery tickets—people are more likely to get that fortune they're looking for by sticking that money into their RRSPs; and
- take lunches to work rather than buying them at pricey delis or restaurants.

"Now, I know a lot of people will resist such 'sacrifices,' and that's fine, as long as they understand what they're really giving up 25 years down the road. When you look at the long term, some of these expensive tastes and daily habits might appeal to you a little less."

Noah didn't start building the ark after it started raining.

— Warren Buffett

ON RETIREMENT PLANS FOR YOUNG PEOPLE

"Everyone who works for a steady income during their lifetime can retire comfortably," said Sara. "One of our society's great failings is that we haven't made retirement planning as prominent as it should be. Other nations are doing much better in this area, and I can only believe that their citizens will realize big payoffs in terms of both individual happiness and their national economies.

"For example, some Asian countries *require* each worker to contribute a fairly hefty percentage of income to individual retirement plans. The money is taken out at the payroll source. In Singapore, for example, workers and employers match contributions—10 percent of their gross income—to enable them to retire with $750,000 in their retirement funds.

"It just makes sense to require people to look after their own retirements throughout their working lives, so they won't be dependent on social programs when they finally do leave the workforce. Our system and many people's procrastination result in a burgeoning national debt and people's dependency on our governments to look after us.

"We have all seen how poor government performance is in planning and budgeting money. It's unbelievable, really, that the CPP currently faces shortfalls unless working Canadians double their contributions. Demographers have known for decades there was a baby-boomer bulge that would mean a huge number of people retiring and becoming a tremendous burden for those fewer people working and making CPP contributions. The ratio is going to be about one retiree for every two working people whereas the ratio in the past has been one retiree to four workers.

"Years ago there was talk about having to take decisive action—but nothing was done. Obviously someone in government wasn't thinking clearly.

"I have to agree," I said. "If there had been legislation dictating that I contribute a certain amount since I began working at age 18, I don't think I'd have any worries at all now. It might be an unpopular move at the time, but I can't see how any thinking person could really object, if, in fact, the money was theirs to compound and keep at retirement."

"Another thing I think Canada should do," said Sara, "is make retirement planning a mandatory course of study for students in senior high school. Ninety-nine percent of the teenagers I've spoken with don't have a clue what they need to do to prepare for retirement. There's this assumption that everything will work out in the end if they start worrying about it when they're older.

"Well, we know you get older awfully fast and waiting is the worst strategy!

"Many young people, particularly those in their twenties who change jobs every few years, cash in retirement funds every time they change employers. To the young who can never conceive of age catching up with them, these funds look like windfalls ripe for the spending. I think the government should prohibit anyone's cashing in a retirement fund before the age of 55, period!

"From the strip-bond scenario we've worked on already you can see easily how that paltry $4,000 invested in a pension fund could grow to $20,000 in 20 years, and to $100,000 in 40 years. Even people making only $20,000 a year can contribute $3,600 a year—$2,556 after a 29 percent tax rebate. If they'd just forget about that money for a few decades, they'd be well off."

"I know what you mean from personal experience," I said. "I took $6,000 out of two work pensions before I was 30 to buy a Malibu hardtop and some other such nonsense. I can see now that that relatively small sum of money would have bought me a Mercedes 500SL by retirement if I'd left it in and got the car at that younger age some other way."

"Oh, so you were one of those shortsighted young people I'm talking about!" said Sara. "Maybe you can do your bit to get that message out to policymakers. Let's work out a scenario for a fictional young person who has foresight. It takes only a few minutes."

"Great," I said. "I have a niece I've been trying to convince to start an RRSP, but she's only 21 and she can't see why she should do anything about it now."

"Well, maybe we can help convince her. We'll have to make some of our famous assumptions again," said Sara. "Let's pretend your twenty-one-year-old niece:

- earns a $20,000 annual salary today that will increase by a modest 2.5 percent each year until she retires at age 65;
- contributes her maximum RRSP allotment of 18 percent per year; and
- that her RRSP savings will compound by 6 percent a year.

"She has 44 years to retirement, so the picture looks like this—"

NIECE'S RRSP PROJECTION TO YEAR 2040

Year	Annual Salary	Salary Increase (%)	RRSP/ Year	RRSP Growth (%)	RRSP Value
1997	$20,000	2.50	$3,600	6.00	$3,816
1998	20,500	2.50	3,690	6.00	7,956
1999	21,013	2.50	3,782	6.00	12,442
2000	21,538	2.50	3,877	6.00	17,298
2001	22,076	2.50	3,974	6.00	22,548
2002	22,628	2.50	4,073	6.00	28,218
2003	23,194	2.50	4,175	6.00	34,337
2004	23,774	2.50	4,279	6.00	40,933
2005	24,368	2.50	4,386	6.00	48,038
2006	24,977	2.50	4,496	6.00	55,686
2007	25,601	2.50	4,608	6.00	63,912
2008	26,241	2.50	4,723	6.00	72,753
2009	26,897	2.50	4,841	6.00	82,250
2010	27,569	2.50	4,962	6.00	92,445
2011	28,258	2.50	5,086	6.00	103,383
2012	28,964	2.50	5,214	6.00	115,113
2013	29,688	2.50	5,344	6.00	127,684
2014	30,430	2.50	5,477	6.00	141,151
2015	31,191	2.50	5,614	6.00	155,571
2016	31,971	2.50	5,755	6.00	171,006
2017	32,770	2.50	5,899	6.00	187,519
2018	33,589	2.50	6,046	6.00	205,179
2019	34,429	2.50	6,197	6.00	224,059
2020	35,290	2.50	6,352	6.00	244,236
2021	36,172	2.50	6,511	6.00	265,792
2022	37,076	2.50	6,674	6.00	288,814
2023	38,003	2.50	6,841	6.00	313,394
2024	38,953	2.50	7,012	6.00	339,630
2025	39,927	2.50	7,187	6.00	367,626
2026	40,925	2.50	7,367	6.00	397,493
2027	41,948	2.50	7,551	6.00	429,347
2028	42,997	2.50	7,739	6.00	463,311
2029	44,072	2.50	7,933	6.00	499,519
2030	45,174	2.50	8,131	6.00	538,109
2031	46,303	2.50	8,335	6.00	579,231
2032	47,461	2.50	8,543	6.00	623,040
2033	48,648	2.50	8,757	6.00	669,705
2034	49,864	2.50	8,976	6.00	719,402
2035	51,111	2.50	9,200	6.00	772,318
2036	52,389	2.50	9,430	6.00	828,653
2037	53,699	2.50	9,666	6.00	888,618
2038	55,041	2.50	9,907	6.00	952,437
2039	56,417	2.50	10,155	6.00	1,020,348
2040	57,827	2.50	10,409	6.00	1,092,602

"Your niece could easily be a millionaire when she retires," continued Sara, "and in her first year of retirement, 2040, she could gross $75,074 if she withdrew only the interest at 6 percent. If she has other pension plans and the CPP, her retirement should be very comfortable indeed.

"It still amazes me, even after all the RRSP scenarios we've run," said Sara. "Your niece, earning a very conservative salary and getting raises that just keep pace with inflation, could easily be a millionaire at retirement even if she played it entirely safe and interest rates never exceeded 6 percent. This is about as conservative a scenario as you can create and it still gets a person to the age of retirement with sufficient funds to live a better lifestyle than he or she could afford during their working life."

> **There is nothing more tragic in life than the utter impossibility of changing what you have done.**
>
> **— John Galsworthy**

A SCENARIO FOR SMALL RRSPS IN MIDLIFE

"Do you think you could bear with me for one more scenario?" I asked, concerned that I might be stretching the limits of Sara's goodwill.

"What kind of scenario?" she asked.

"Oh, it's an easy one. After this, I promise I'll try to do them myself. I think you and Gordon have presented compelling cases for myself and Lorraine, and for my niece. I wonder, though, if you can do your wizardry for a friend who has been even more of a procrastinator than we've been. This could be tougher, given that he has much less in an RRSP."

"The same process can apply to anyone's situation," said Sara, "but if someone doesn't make a serious effort to put money away, no amount of strategizing is going to secure a comfortable

157

retirement. People have to make informed and deliberate choices, and someone who doesn't have a good work pension, who chooses not to save, and who assumes CPP alone is going to provide any kind of lifestyle, may have to dance to a not-so-pleasant tune in retirement.

"But that's kind of negative," she said. "I think we could do a quicky analysis of your friend's situation and you can go through it with him when you get back. You must be getting the feel for this."

"I hope so!" I said. "It really is great of you to take all this time. We should do something to make it worth your while."

"I'll have received more than enough reward if I help prepare you so you never need anyone like me again. It reminds me of something my father used to say: 'Your first priority should be to acquire the knowledge you need to manage your own life. By doing your own thinking you will save the expense of having to hire others to do your thinking for you.'

"So, consider this all assistance with that priority. Now, for your friend. Question number one," Sara said, "has to be how much has he put away so far?"

"Not much," I confessed. "He says only about $20,000 and he's 40 years old."

"Will he have a company pension?" asked Gordon.

"I don't think so. He's a fisherman and there's no plan with the people who own the boat."

"Okay," said Sara. "So we have $20,000 and 25 years to age 65. Does he own a home?"

"A condominium, and he says there are 15 years to go on the mortgage."

"What's its value?" asked Gordon.

"He thinks about $150,000, and it's hard to say if that figure will increase much, given the current glut of apartments on the market in the Lower Mainland."

"All right," he said. "We'll have to make some assumptions, as we did with your situation. Let's start with what his RRSP could look like in 25 years starting with the $20,000 he has now. What kind of annual income does he make?"

"It's up and down, as fishing is," I said, "but he's averaged about $30,000 for the past decade."

"So, that means he could contribute $5,400 a year using the 18-percent RRSP contribution rate. Let's see where that will get him using our standard assumption that a person can earn 6-percent interest. What's his name?"

"Gary," I said.

"This should be interesting," said Sara. "His RRSP situation is about as low as it can get for someone his age. Plus he has no work pension, so if we can figure out how he can make it, almost anyone should be able to do it."

She began writing and poking at her calculator. I had to admit she was fast at this. Within moments she handed me a sheet of paper.

GARY'S RRSP PROJECTION TO YEAR 2022

Year	Amount Invested	Return Rate (%)	Interest Earned	Year End Value	New Investment
1997	$20,000	6.00	$1,200	$21,200	$5,400
1998	26,600	6.00	1,596	28,196	5,400
1999	33,596	6.00	2,016	35,612	5,400
2000	41,012	6.00	2,461	43,472	5,400
2001	48,872	6.00	2,932	51,805	5,400
2002	57,205	6.00	3,432	60,637	5,400
2003	66,037	6.00	3,962	69,999	5,400
2004	75,399	6.00	4,524	79,923	5,400
2005	85,323	6.00	5,119	90,443	5,400
2006	95,843	6.00	5,751	101,593	5,400
2007	106,993	6.00	6,420	113,413	5,400
2008	118,813	6.00	7,129	125,942	5,400
2009	131,342	6.00	7,881	139,222	5,400
2010	144,622	6.00	8,677	153,299	5,400
2011	158,699	6.00	9,522	168,221	5,400
2012	173,621	6.00	10,418	184,039	5,400
2013	189,439	6.00	11,366	200,805	5,400
2014	206,205	6.00	12,372	218,577	5,400
2015	223,977	6.00	13,439	237,416	5,400
2016	242,816	6.00	14,569	257,385	5,400
2017	262,785	6.00	15,767	278,552	5,400
2018	283,952	6.00	17,037	300,989	5,400
2019	306,389	6.00	18,383	324,773	5,400
2020	330,173	6.00	19,810	349,983	5,400
2021	355,383	6.00	21,323	376,706	5,400
2022	382,106	6.00	22,926	405,032	5,400

"Boy!" I said after reading the sheet. "He doesn't look quite so badly off at retirement."

"Not quite so bad," said Sara, "but we're not finished. Saving the $5,400 a year works out to $450 a month. That might seem like a lot on his $30,000 salary—only about $20,000 of which is take home—but he gets a third of the $450 back at tax time from making the RRSP contribution, so it's really only $315 a month."

"Still, the interest on the $405,032 wouldn't be sufficient to live any kind of decent lifestyle. So we'd better make some more assumptions. As I see it, he has several options that will help. First, he'll receive CPP if it's there, and we'll assume it will be; second, he will sell his apartment and move to a retirement village to free up the capital.

"He'd be able to earn $24,302 in interest each year from his RRIF without touching his capital if he simply leaves it in something safe at 6-percent annual interest.

"Next, let's look at what CPP should be worth in the year 2022. The government has indicated it may de-index CPP to the point that it inflates at 1 percent below the rate of inflation. So, if we assume inflation will be 2.5 percent per year, CPP benefits will grow by only 1.5 percent. So, in the year 2021 the maximum CPP entitlement of $713 today will be worth . . ."

She resumed her poking.

"$1,034 per month. Is he married?"

"No, a confirmed bachelor."

"Oh, boy," said Sara. "Well, his income from his RRIF interest will be $24,302 gross, and his CPP will add $12,408 for a total of $36,710—not an impossibly low amount to live on today, but that 2.5-percent inflation is going to hurt him. Let's get his other income option into the picture before I calculate the damage.

"Let's assume Vancouver prices are going to escalate a bit with the continued influx of immigrants and other people from across Canada who want the warmer climate. He should be looking at about $200,000 in 15 years, maybe more since apartments may fare better than houses. In fact, he might do quite well if a lot of the people selling their houses opt for lower-cost apartments.

"Now, let's assume he can exchange his $200,000 from his Vancouver home for something worth $150,000 in a smaller center. That gives him another $50,000 to collect interest on. Using our 6-percent figure again, that's another $3,000 per year, so his total annual income rises to $39,710."

"Still not great," I said, "particularly given current inflation."

"No, but we're not down and out yet. We haven't touched his principal and he'd have $455,032 there that he may as well not take to the grave. He obviously isn't living a rich lifestyle now and he may have to continue the same level of existence. Let's assume he needs $2,000 a month to live on now and that he can continue with the equivalent of that for the rest of his life.

"By extrapolating 2.5-percent inflation, we see what he'll need in the year he begins retirement at 2022. We'll hope he dies at age 80 as he's supposed to!"

"I'm sure he'll appreciate that," I said.

More poking on the calculator.

"The $2,000 today comes to $3,707 per month in 2022. We have to assume this sum will have to grow by the same 2.5 percent per year to keep him solvent. Let's run a scenario."

More poking. Her fingers must have been getting sore.

"Okay, he'll need at least $3,707 net a month, or $44,484 a year in 2022 ($62,654 gross income). His interest and CPP will provide only $39,710 gross, $28,194 net at a 29-percent tax rate. We have a gross income deficit in year one of $22,944."

Poke, poke.

"So he needs to withdraw from his principal $22,944 in year one. Let's see what happens when we inflate what he needs by 2.5 percent a year and start running down his principal so he doesn't die a rich man. For ease of calculation we'll assume he earns interest on the entire principal balance each year.

"Uh-hmm. The $3,707 per month will have to grow to $5,369 by the year he dies, 2037. So now we can start running down his principal each year to give him pretty close to what we think he'll need. Just to confuse things, we'll also inflate his CPP by the same 1.5 percent we assumed earlier.

GARY'S DRAW-DOWN OF HIS RRIF, 2022 TO 2037

Year	Principal	Interest	CPP	Required Income	Draw-down
2022	$455,032	$27,302	$12,408	$62,654	$22,944
2023	432,088	25,925	12,594	64,220	25,701
2024	406,387	24,383	12,783	65,826	28,660
2025	377,727	22,664	12,975	67,472	31,833
2026	345,894	20,754	13,170	69,159	35,235
2027	310,659	18,640	13,368	70,888	38,880
2028	271,779	16,307	13,569	72,660	42,784
2029	228,995	13,740	13,773	74,477	46,964
2030	182,031	10,922	13,980	76,339	51,437
2031	130,594	7,836	14,190	78,247	56,221
2032	74,373	4,462	14,403	80,203	61,338
2033	13,035	782	14,619	82,208	(66,807)
2034			14,838	84,263	
2035			15,061	86,370	
2036			15,287	88,529	
2037			15,516	90,742	

Interest on principal @ 6% annually and calculated at start of year.
CPP inflates by 1.5% per year.
Required gross income inflates by 2.5% each year.
Draw-down is adjusted to produce required income.

"We know he needs $5,369 net a month to maintain his lifestyle in 2037, and that would be a gross income of about $91,000 a year. He comes up a bit short as of 2033," said Sara.

"So, should I go back and tell him to die a few years earlier?"

"Well, that's one option," said Sara, "but not if you want to keep your friends. I wish that more people would run these scenarios so planning for the future isn't just groping around in the dark."

"Why, so they can get depressed?"

"No, wise guy. So they can see realistically where they may be lacking while they still have 25 years to do something about it. Even with a small amount of money in his RRSP now, Gary can retire well if he takes the right steps."

"What do you think he can do?"

"He has several options I can think of immediately. I hope you can convince him he has to do something. He needs to. He could consider:

1. Retiring at 67 to allow his RRSP to compound for two more years. Delaying his retirement this long would start him off with $466,885 instead of the $405,032. So, he would have $61,853 more on which to earn interest and two years less to draw his principal down.

2. He could consider putting more money away now outside his RRSP since he's already making maximum contributions. If he sacrificed a bit for the next few years, he could build up a nest egg outside his RRSP that could also grow, albeit within the taxman's reach.

3. He could get a part-time job when he's not fishing. This would produce two results: a) give him a higher income and thus more room to contribute to his RRSP; and b) more money to save. Even getting a part-time job for a few years would help his situation as his contributions would benefit from the compounding when he's still a couple of decades away from 65.

4. He could make darn sure he's got some entrepreneurial skills and knowledge to enable him to earn some income when he's retired. The problem with counting on this option too much is that it would tempt Gary to procrastinate rather than do something now. He could also find himself disabled in retirement and unable to do the work he thought he could do. Far better to pursue options 1 through 3 while he still can.

Another Option

"There is another seldom-discussed option that some Canadians are going to pursue in the future," said Sara, "—retirement outside Canada. For some reason, most people automatically assume they will retire in Canada and escape to some safe American state, like Hawaii or Arizona, for just a few weeks or months each year. That's all right if that's really the extent of your imagination, but there's a whole world out there! And being a slave to a health-care system and feeling comfortable only among people who speak English is limiting both personally and financially.

"Consider that a person today with a $40,000 income could live like a king or queen in a dozen countries around the world where the weather is good, and crime and pollution are minimal. People just don't know about them because few of us ever get off the usual tourist tracks.

"I raise this because I think people who can't or don't save sufficient funds to live decently in Canada in the coming decades can make their money go further in retirement by finding a suitable developing country where the dollar goes as much as five times further. Of course, we don't know exactly what these countries are going to be like in 20 or 30 years, and it's entirely possible the 100 million retiring North Americans, plus another few hundred million Europeans, will seek them out first, make them much better known and crowded and perhaps even more expensive.

"I am willing to bet, however, that at any time over the next 40 years, you'll be able to find very nice places to holiday that won't be a threat to mind or body. If I were you I'd start looking now and have the best ones scouted out before you retire.

"At any rate, that's another topic. Back to where we are. Does all this stuff for Gary make sense to you?"

"Yes! I only hope Gary takes the advice in the spirit in which it will be intended," I said. "How many friends have you lost by telling them to save more money and get a second job?"

"Actually, we try not to counsel anyone who doesn't request it," said Sara. "Even though all this stuff makes perfect sense because it's simple mathematics, a lot of people prefer not to think about it. It does involve discipline and even some sacrifices. For some reason some people always assume everything's going to work out for them. In the years when you're working and young, things always do seem to work out, but once you're older and on a fixed income, living on wishes and hopes can be a bit dangerous.

"But, my friend, just in case you want to lose some friends of your own, I thought I'd give you a typical planning worksheet to take home and photocopy. Then, whenever someone has been a friend for too long, you can whip it out, crunch some numbers, and lose them forever. In fact, to ensure you can do it with your eyes opened or closed, let's have you run through two scenarios."

"What scenarios?" I asked.

"Well, let's pick two that could be useful to other segments of society that traditionally have a lot of difficulty planning for a financially comfortable retirement. Let's do a couple in their thirties with two kids, and then a single mother receiving a minimum wage. Millions of Canadians fit these descriptions and the exercise should be instructive. So, how do you propose to start?"

"I guess, to follow examples set by brilliant friends of mine, I'd better make some assumptions about income, inflation, RRSP contribution sums, and the growth of the RRSPs.

"For the couple with two children, let's suppose the husband earns $30,000 a year and the wife, earning only the $7.50 minimum wage, grosses $13,650 per year. At the 18-percent contribution maximum, this means the husband can contribute $5,400 to an RRSP and the wife $2,457, a total of $7,857 a year, or $655 a month.

"From what I know about the cost of raising kids, I can speculate right now that people earning less than $44,000 combined incomes will have trouble putting away $655 a month. I understand they would get a tax rebate for the RRSP contribution of about 30 percent, or $2,357, so that reduces what they actually contribute to their RRSPs to $5,500 but that's still $458 a month, a lot of money for people who net only about $2,550 a month."

"You're right," said Sara. "It would represent a lot of money and people living on this level of income must face that. It would be nicer if everyone earned sufficient funds so that saving for retirement wasn't a strain, but that's not the way it is. Actually people have a lot of choices. They can:

1. Do nothing and rely on government retirement programs when they reach retirement age (in 35 years, the maximum monthly CPP benefit today, $713, inflated by 1.5 percent annually would pay $1,200 per month per person).
2. Put some money into RRSPs—as much as they can afford each year.
3. Wait until later in life when they can more easily afford to contribute to retirement plans. Or,
4. Bite the bullet and contribute the maximum to retirement plans by learning to live with less money while they raise their children.

"At age 65 I know which option people will wish they'd chosen, but this is your scenario, so which one do you want to work with?"

"Well, we know the maximum they need to save, after the tax rebate, is $458 a month. That's about $315 for the husband and $143 for the wife. Break it down into bi-weekly paydays and the sums are $157.50 and $71.50 respectively. I know many people like to look at the total figure, before the tax rebate, or in this case the $655 number, but that's even more depressing and makes the concept more psychologically daunting.

"The reality is that you do get that money back and it takes only one year of planning to build it into the lifelong scenario. I agree with you that people who really want to do something great for their retirement must be prepared to make some level of sacrifice. I believe the strategy must be to plan a budget carefully and then see if they maintain the level of life they consider reasonable. If they can manage it, get those RRSP deductions made 'at payroll source' and just forget about them for several decades. Once you learn to live without the money and stop thinking about it, you'll find things get much easier.

"But, what I think is doable may seem totally unfeasible to someone else. Let's suppose this thirty-year-old couple can only save half of their allowable maximum. In other words, although they *could* put away $7,857, let's assume they save only $3,928, or $327 per month. Still a lot of money for some people, but they'll get back about $100 as a tax rebate, so the real out-of-pocket is only about $227 per month.

"And, given that they will, in all likelihood, receive annual raises, we'll increase the RRSP contribution by 2.5 percent each year, and we'll grow the total compounding contributions by the usual 6 percent. This means in year one, 1997, they begin, both at age 30, with $3,928. They'll retire in 2031."

My turn to poke.

RRSP CONTRIBUTIONS FOR THIRTY-SOMETHING COUPLE, 1997 TO 2031

Begin 1997 with annual contribution of $3,928 earning 6% interest. Each subsequent year sees RRSP contributions increase by 2.5% and also earn 6% interest.

Year	Amount Invested	Return Rate (%)	Year End Value	New Investment
1997	$3,928	6.00	$4,164	$4,026
1998	8,190	6.00	8,681	4,127
1999	12,808	6.00	13,576	4,230
2000	17,806	6.00	18,874	4,336
2001	23,210	6.00	24,603	4,444
2002	29,047	6.00	30,790	4,555
2003	35,345	6.00	37,466	4,669
2004	42,135	6.00	44,663	4,786
2005	49,449	6.00	52,416	4,906
2006	57,322	6.00	60,761	5,029
2007	65,790	6.00	69,737	5,155
2008	74,892	6.00	79,386	5,284
2009	84,670	6.00	89,750	5,416
2010	95,166	6.00	100,876	5,551
2011	106,427	6.00	112,813	5,690
2012	118,503	6.00	125,613	5,832
2013	131,445	6.00	139,332	5,978
2014	145,310	6.00	154,029	6,127
2015	160,156	6.00	169,765	6,280
2016	176,045	6.00	186,608	6,437
2017	193,045	6.00	204,628	6,598
2018	211,226	6.00	223,900	6,763
2019	230,663	6.00	244,503	6,932
2020	251,435	6.00	266,521	7,105
2021	273,626	6.00	290,044	7,283
2022	297,327	6.00	315,167	7,465
2023	322,632	6.00	341,990	7,652
2024	349,642	6.00	370,621	7,843
2025	378,464	6.00	401,172	8,039
2026	409,211	6.00	433,764	8,240
2027	442,004	6.00	468,524	8,446
2028	476,970	6.00	505,588	8,657
2029	514,245	6.00	545,100	8,873
2030	553,973	6.00	587,211	9,095
2031	596,306	6.00	632,084	9,322

(1997 x 2.5?)

169

As usual, by the end of the calculations, I was surprised by the final number. Two people, both 30, with two kids and earning only an average income and making only half of their allowable contributions, could retire with $632,000 in the bank. And this assuming they never increased their contributions when the children were grown, and that they earned a fairly conservative return on their RRSPs. For anyone at all serious about saving for retirement, this must represent pretty much a worst-case scenario.

From all of Sara's and Gordon's previous scenarios in recent days I could quickly envision the annual-income picture, including taking into account a draw-down on principal to conform with RRIF requirements:

- 6% interest on the 2031 balance   = $37,925
- plus some principal draw-down   = $20,000
- CPP for 2 people, estimate   = <u>$28,800</u>
  Total combined income   = <u>**$86,725**</u>

Granted, this gross figure of $86,725 won't buy nearly as much in the year 2031, but look at the alternative of trying to live on only the CPP alone—$28,800—plus whatever the Seniors' Benefit pays in 35 years, if anything.

So, that's what a couple making a bit of effort could do. I wondered aloud to Sara how someone 30 years old earning nothing but minimum wage—$13,650 per year—could fare.

"It doesn't sound pretty given the gross monthly wage would total only $1,138," she said, "and I'm sure this is why many single mothers or fathers paying child support think it's a waste of time. Still, I like your idea. Why not run the numbers to see if a person with a very low income could accumulate any kind of retirement fund? You're pretty quick at this, so it shouldn't take long to find out. What assumptions are you going to make?"

"Well, first of all, given the low wage I think I'll try $25 a paycheck. Over 26 pay days, that would total $650 a year. To ease the pain the person would get $189 of that back (at a 29% tax bracket) so the real first-year annual contribution would be only $461. I'll grow the RRSP contribution by the 2.5 percent and the RRSP compounding at six percent. Again, we have 35 years to accumulate the fund."

I began jabbing at the calculator.

RRSP CONTRIBUTIONS FOR MINIMUM-WAGE EARNER, 1997 TO 2031

Begin 1997 with contribution of $650 earning 6% interest. Each subsequent year sees RRSP contributions increased by 2.5% and also earning 6% interest.

Year	RRSP Compounded	Year	RRSP Compounded
1997	$ 689	2015	$28,091
1998	1,437	2016	30,878
1999	2,247	2017	33,859
2000	3,123	2018	37,048
2001	4,071	2019	40,457
2002	5,095	2020	44,101
2003	6,200	2021	47,993
2004	7,391	2022	52,150
2005	8,674	2023	56,588
2006	10,055	2024	61,325
2007	11,540	2025	66,381
2008	13,137	2026	71,773
2009	14,851	2027	77,525
2010	16,682	2028	83,658
2011	18,667	2029	90,196
2012	20,785	2030	97,164
2013	23,055	2031	104,589
2014	25,487		

"Not so good on this one," I said, after sharing the bottom line with Sara.

"Well, think about that," she said. "Ask yourself what this fictional person will earn per year *without* that RRSP."

"Okay. We know CPP, inflated by 1.5 percent per year from today's $713 figure will gross a person $1,200 per month, or about $14,400 per year. We don't know, of course, about the Seniors' Benefit or what will be in place in the year 2031."

"So we have a person aged 65 with a guaranteed $14,400 from CPP. Now, what if you commit to taking $10,000 each year from the RRSP/RRIF reserve using a combination of interest and principal? This would meet RRIF draw-down requirements. See what age the person would be before the RRSP ran out."

I started stabbing again.

PRINCIPAL AND INTEREST "RUNDOWN"

Annual interest accumulates at 6%
Draw-down $10,000/year

Age	Year	Open Value	Gross Payment per period	Withholding Tax per period	Net Payment per period	Total Net Annual Payment
65	2031	$104,589	$10,000	$2,000	$8,000	$8,000
66	2032	100,264	10,000	1,198	8,802	8,802
67	2033	95,680	10,000	1,202	8,797	8,797
68	2034	90,821	10,000	1,210	8,790	8,790
69	2035	85,670	10,000	1,221	8,779	8,779
70	2036	80,210	10,000	1,236	8,764	8,764
71	2037	74,423	10,000	1,256	8,744	8,744
72	2038	68,289	10,000	496	9,504	9,504
73	2039	61,786	10,000	1,076	8,924	8,924
74	2040	54,893	10,000	1,167	8,833	8,833
75	2041	47,587	10,000	1,266	8,734	8,734
76	2042	39,842	10,000	1,374	8,626	8,626
77	2043	31,632	10,000	1,495	8,505	8,506
78	2044	22,930	10,000	1,626	8,374	8,374
79	2045	13,706	10,000	1,772	8,228	8,228
80	2046	3,928	3,928	359	3,569	3,569

Note: The start date for payment is the 1st day of the year he/she turns 65.

At age 80 the person would be out of RRIF funds, but I could see some real positives to the plan even so.

Sara saw them too. "So, what do you think?"

"I think, if I were this person, I'd sooner have that extra $10,000 a year for even 15 years than not have it. It could make the difference between a subsistence retirement and one with *some* extras."

"Quite right," said Sara. "I think there're a few more statistics worth looking at to prove that even a person on minimum wage able to contribute only $25 per payday, growing by 2.5% per year, is very wise to do so. Okay, calculate how much money the person actually contributed from earnings."

I poked away to add up the 35 years of contributions.

"The contributions totaled $35,709."

"All right," she said, "now deduct 29 percent from that in view of the tax rebate the person would receive each year."

I did. "The tax rebate totaled $10,356, so the real contribution over the 35 years was only $25,353."

"Interesting. Now calculate how much the person actually draws from the RRIF until it's expired."

More jabbing.

"We know the person took $10,000 a year for 15 years and that there would be $3,569 remaining in the year 2046, so the total accumulated and withdrawn would be $153,569."

"Not bad for a $25,353 investment," said Sara. "By putting away only $25 every two weeks a 30-year-old can almost match the funds that CPP will pay. I think I'd rather have almost twice the money at retirement age."

"Ditto," I said.

PERSONAL WORKSHEET

1. Begin 1998, as of January 1, with your intended RRSP contribution.
2. Multiply the number by 6% to add one year's interest.
3. Inflate your 1998 contribution by 2.5% to show your 1999 contribution.
4. Add your 1998 figure to your 1999 contribution and multiply both by 6%.
5. Repeat the process of inflating each subsequent year's contribution by 2.5%, add that figure to the previous year's cumulative total and multiply the total by 6%. See examples on previous pages for guidance.

Year	RRSP Compounded	Year	RRSP Compounded
1998	$	2019	$
1999		2020	
2000		2021	
2001		2022	
2002		2023	
2003		2024	
2004		2025	
2005		2026	
2006		2027	
2007		2028	
2008		2029	
2009		2030	
2010		2031	
2011		2032	
2012		2033	
2013		2034	
2014		2035	
2015		2036	
2016		2037	
2017		2038	
2018		2039	
		2040	

*   *   *

Now my brain *was* tired. I'd been exposed to more life and financial planning information in the past three days than in my entire life. I tossed my papers on the table and pleaded, "Have you got a cold beer?"

"You bet," said Sara, "but only one for you. Gordon wants your mind functioning for a meeting he wants to take you to tonight."

"A meeting?" I asked. "Do I have to think any more?"

"Well, you have to listen, but you don't have to say anything if you don't want to."

"Okay, what's the meeting about?" I asked.

"Investing in stocks," said Sara. "People from The Resort arranged to host a well-known investment counselor traveling through the area doing seminars a while back. I've read some of his stuff and I like him. He has a commonsense approach anyone can follow. We've read a lot of books on stock investing but both Gordon and I get lost between the technical analysts and the fundamentalists.

"You don't have to have securities expertise to follow Wade. He deliberately tailors his approaches so average folk can understand them and use them. And I'm really average!

"Let's go in for supper now, and we'll see what you think later."

The stock market is only a reference to see if anyone is offering to do something foolish.

— Warren Buffett

CHAPTER 7

Stock Approaches For an Edge (SAFE)

Chapter Goal: To present an effective commonsense means of selecting stocks that anyone can master, without investing a great deal of time or money.

DAY 3, Early Evening

As soon as we walked through the door of the kitchen the spicy smell of curry enveloped us.

"I hope you like hot food," said Gordon, our chef for the evening.

"The hotter the better," I said. "I like it when my head sweats."

"Did you know that researchers have found hot foods become quite addictive to some people because they make the brain produce extra endorphins?"

"You mean we get high eating curry?" I asked.

"Sort of. The endorphins are the same as the ones produced while jogging."

"'High' and 'jogging' aren't words I use in the same breath," I said. "I like the idea of food producing a high, though. Maybe it can replace my exercise program."

"What exercise program?" chided Gordon, pinching the little roll of fat around my stomach.

"The one I'm planning to get around to," I said. "Hey, I don't have all day to get healthy like some of my retired friends. I've got to earn a living."

"Yeah, well you'd better think about investing in your body at the same time as your RRSPs, or your wife may end up a very rich widow."

"Boy, you really know how to spoil a guy's appetite," I said.

Supper, like all the other meals I'd had at The Resort, was superb. Tonight, Gordon had conjured up an interesting mixture of Thai dishes: a clear spicy soup, curried chicken with aspara-gus, meatballs in a coconut-milk sauce, rice, steamed vegetables, and a dollop of mango ice cream to finish.

I hoped I wouldn't fall asleep at the meeting.

About an hour after we'd eaten we made our way to "the hall." About 50 people milled around the large meeting room and around the rows of chairs and tables facing a lectern. Obviously, other villagers had invited friends and relatives, too.

A man Gordon identified as the guest speaker, Wade Farthing, was circulating, shaking hands and prompting outbursts of laugh-ter wherever he went. As the clock approached 7 o'clock one of the villagers went to the lectern to call the group to their seats.

Wade Farthing began.

"I'm glad to see a range of age groups in the audience. What I have to say tonight will benefit everyone, I hope, but it can be most valuable for the younger people in the room. They are the ones with the most time to put investment plans to work. Let me start with a question: 'How many of you own stocks now or have invested in them in the past?' A show of hands, please."

About half the people in the room raised their hands.

"How many of you have had more winners than losers from these investments?"

Nervous titters all around. Only a few hands went up.

"Well, the rest of you shouldn't feel too bad, you're in good company. Very few stock-market investors are honestly able to say they do well. Does anyone want to suggest why?"

One man put his hand up.

"It's just my opinion," started the man somewhat shyly, "but I would guess it's because people pick the wrong stocks."

"Well, that may sound obvious to everyone here, but you're absolutely right, my friend. People consistently pick the wrong stocks. Do you have an opinion about why they pick the wrong stocks?"

"I guess it's because they don't know how to pick the *right* stocks."

"My friend, I'm going to sign you to accompany me on these jaunts. Your comments are the most poignant summary I've ever heard to describe how people who invest in stocks lose money. Let me repeat what you said, and I'd ask everybody to think carefully about exactly what you said because you've captured in two sentences the entire essence of what I'm going to say tonight: *People pick the wrong stocks. People don't know how to pick the right stocks.*

"Something that sounds like such a simple dilemma should be easy to fix, right?

"Well, it is and it isn't. I believe making better choices is within everyone's grasp even if you don't have an investor's technical expertise. I know just as certainly that most of the people in this room will likely forget what I say tonight or ignore it. To them I say, the next time you start to question the performance of your stock portfolio or start to think stocks are a mug's game, think back to tonight and dig out some of the papers I'm going to give you. It's never too late to improve your investment strategies. For some reason, most stock investors think their guts and their instincts are somehow smarter than their brains. I'm going to try to change any minds tonight that place their trust in guts and instinct."

He switched on an overhead machine and the following message shone against a sunny yellow backdrop:

To Make Money in Stocks, you need 3 things:

1. Patience.

2. Money you can afford to lose.

3. Knowledge to lessen the likelihood of #2 occurring.

"I can't give you patience," said Farthing, "although I can suggest that if you don't have it, try to develop it. And I can't give you money to lose. What I do hope I can give you is number three, or at least the beginning of a plan that you can fine-tune yourself.

"Let me begin by saying we could all do worse than to follow investment advice from Warren Buffett, arguably the world's greatest stock investor. Buffett is an anomaly in the investment world. He buys companies that appear to others to be in fiscal tatters and he holds stocks while other investors sell in a panic.

"In fact, he rarely sells, preferring instead to buy quality companies and hold them for years while their stock values steadily rise. He says about 12 stocks have made his fortune, and even though his company, Berkshire Hathaway, is worth billions, there are usually only about 10 companies in his portfolio. And most of those have been there for more than a decade.

"Buffett's buy-and-hold strategy is dramatized exquisitely through one simple example contained on the first sheet I'm going to pass out tonight."

He handed a package of photocopied sheets to the man chairing the meeting and the sheets were distributed to everyone.

"Take a few minutes to read and think about the information."

THE POWER OF "BUY AND HOLD"

Suppose you are a stock buyer who believes in buying for the short term and selling when your stocks hit a predetermined sell target. Look at what happens to the value of an investment in 4 examples. In each one the initial purchase is one $1 stock. This single stock doubles in value each year over a 20-year period. The difference in the scenarios is that two investors sell their "doubled" stock each year and buy another stock that also doubles over the next year. The other two investors buy and hold.

See what happens:

1. Outside an RRSP, flipping doubled stock every year.

A stock worth $1 doubles in year 1. Tax and brokerage fees are paid at a combined rate of 21% (17% for capital gain and 2% brokerage fee for each buy/sell transaction). The remaining proceeds are then reinvested and this stock again doubles. This process repeats itself for 20 years with tax and brokerage fees paid on each annual gain and brokerage buy/sell. This investor nets about $11,255 over the 20 years on the original $1 investment.

2. Inside an RRSP, flipping doubled stock every year.

The same stock, still doubling annually and bought and sold each year, but totally tax-sheltered, would net you about $467,171 as an RRSP investor after you pay only the 2% brokerage fee on each annual buy-and-sell transaction—4% total.

3. Outside an RRSP, single stock held 20 years, and doubling each year.

A single stock, doubling every year and "held," would be worth $1,048,575 gross in 20 years; taxes are paid on 75% of the gain ($786,432) at a combined federal/provincial tax rate of 47%—in this case $369,623. The investor nets $678,953.

4. Inside an RRSP, single stock held 20 years, doubles each year.

The investor nets the entire gain of $1,048,575. The previous example #2 shows that the brokerage fees alone, at 2 percent for each annual buy-and-sell transaction, would cost the frequent buy-and-sell RRSP investor $581,404 over a 20-year period. The non-RRSP "flipping" investor who is forced to pay annual taxes and brokerage fees loses $667,698 when compared to the non-RRSP "holder."

Wade Farthing waited a few minutes. "Okay. Is there anyone in the room who has a different perspective on the continuous churning of stocks? Feel free to disagree with me. Different perspectives make for a more interesting evening, and I doubt everyone agrees with my view."

No disagreement so far. I had to admit he made his argument pretty forcefully on that single sheet of paper.

"All right," he continued, "let's take a look at the stock market and how people approach it. I'll start with this." Another overhead was displayed.

THE STOCK MARKET: IT'S NOT A MONOPOLY

"I contend that you, as an investor, should have good, clear, and precise reasons for buying every stock you buy, and that the 'buy' decision should be driven by facts, not driven by your instinct or gut.

"It's amazing how some people use money, RRSPs in particular, as though buying equities were a game of monopoly. Perhaps it's because RRSPs don't seem like 'real' money to someone 20 years from retirement, so taking risks doesn't seem 'real.' The problem with this way of thinking, of course, is that losses within an RRSP are 'real' and they can never be made up or mitigated.

"Why?

"Because the government doesn't allow people to replace RRSP losses. Also, these losses aren't even tax-deductible as they would be if the money were lost as an investment outside an RRSP. For these two reasons it makes absolutely no sense to play monopoly with your RRSP funds. If you want to take significant gambles, do it outside your RRSP."

Another overhead:

HOW DID THE GAME GET STARTED?

"The monopoly game started in the early 1990s as people began shifting in droves from lackluster interest-bearing instruments into the booming equities. Brokers report that many people have taken six-figure sums of money and decided to buy 10 to 20 stocks in only a few hours—often these buy decisions were based solely on an analyst's recommendations about what had been doing well recently or stocks that his "gut" thought should do well. Frequently, an investor will devote less than half a day to picking companies—as though there were some time limit to get the $100,000 into the market!

"Warren Buffett's approach deserves consideration. He proposes stock investors approach the process as though they have a license to purchase only a certain number of stocks in their lifetime—say 20. Each time you decide to purchase a stock, you have one stock less you can buy over your entire lifetime.

"Buffett's contention is that stock investing shouldn't mirror draw poker where you continually throw away cards because you don't like them and then take more cards, which, of course, you may decide you don't like, either.

"One thing I'd like to add to clarify that the buy-and-hold strategy doesn't apply to all stocks. Specifically, it doesn't apply to cyclical stocks that follow certain patterns over economic growth cycles.

"For example, lumber- and paper-producing companies are cyclicals that do well when economies are growing, when new house starts spike dramatically, or when advertisers are bullish and newspapers expand in size from greatly increased ad revenues.

"Astute investors buy and sell cyclical stocks according to the economy's direction. For example, you shouldn't count on forestry company stocks rising when interest rates are high, consumer confidence is low, and relatively few people are willing to accept the risk of a large mortgage from building a new house.

"If you want to deal in cyclicals, study and understand all the stages of the stocks' cycles. Ideally have some intelligent contacts in the particular industry, or industries, too, so you have a real feel for where things are now and where they might be in six or nine months.

"Continuing the analysis of cyclicals, and the forestry sector in particular, investors watching the economy and marketplace in 1992 would have seen rapid growth in almost all sectors and an optimism not seen since the mid-eighties. Interest rates started dropping rapidly and the stock markets took off in lock-step with new construction. From the end of 1992 to the end of 1993, almost every forestry company trading on the Toronto

Stock Exchange saw their stocks appreciate by 30 to 100 percent in that single year. If you held for another year, however, you would have seen all or almost all of that gain lost."

WHEN BUY AND HOLD MAKES SENSE

"Buy and hold does make sense, however, with other types of companies, specifically those that provide products or services that are needed by other industries or the masses during good times and bad. Companies like Coca-Cola, Gillette, some fast-food franchises, and the best discount retail stores will continue to do well in good and bad economic cycles.

"Look also for companies that have good global growth prospects that lessen dependence on Canada's or North America's economy—Northern Telecom and Bombardier are two companies that have positioned themselves well to benefit from expanding global markets."

Wade Farthing stopped talking long enough to project the words for another overhead:

THE MOST IMPORTANT LESSON YOU CAN LEARN TONIGHT

EVERY STOCK PURCHASE SHOULD BE THE RESULT OF SYSTEMATIC RESEARCH

"Let me repeat that. If you learn nothing else tonight, it should be that each stock choice should be the culmination of considerable time and research. *After* you've done the necessary homework, you can be much more confident about your decisions and won't be as likely to get 'scared out' of a stock just because of a price dip. If it's a good stock and your research continues to support your initial decision to buy it, chances are the stock will recover in days, weeks, or months.

"Now, I know I've mentioned research several times tonight

and the usual response of people is something like: 'oh God, I don't know anything about research,' or, 'Geez, research, that sounds painful, do I have to?'

"My answer is, of course you don't have to, but if you don't do it you might as well throw darts at the stock page and pick the stocks you hit.

"I contend that even small investors, those of you with only a few thousand dollars and no financial background, can easily and inexpensively sift through a small amount of information to find one or two companies with good fundamentals and good prospects for the future.

"I'm going to tell you precisely what to look for tonight, but first I want to cover a few more general market concepts."

Another overhead:

BUY STRENGTH OR WEAKNESS

"You can buy on strength and you can buy on weakness. Either way you must be informed about your reasons for doing so.

"It can be wise to buy stocks on the way up, if you have assembled information that indicates the particular company is likely to continue to grow. If revenues continue to grow, earnings continue to improve, and costs are controlled, the market will ultimately reward the stock and the upward momentum can well go on until the fundamentals get ahead of themselves. When this happens it's time to sell.

"If you ignore the need for research, though, and don't foresee the decline in revenues, the drop in earnings, or watch financial reports to spot costs getting out of control (so that profits fall), the market will punish the stock. In these cases, wait for the basics to get back into shape and then consider buying, but not until everything adds up.

"The markets in both Canada and the U.S. have been very

STOCK APPROACHES FOR AN EDGE (SAFE)

nervous in recent years. Companies that report downturns in their earnings, even for a quarter, frequently get hammered. So, if a particular stock price is driven largely by earnings, you want to be awfully confident those earnings are going to continue to rise."

Another overhead:

BUYING ON WEAKNESS

"Buying on weakness can be another good strategy, but it takes courage and confidence in the quality of your research. Again, accessing information is the key. Companies that suffer dramatic stock devaluations sometimes deserve the price drop because:"

Another overhead:

- **The future isn't bright for revenues or earnings,**
- **Debt loads are excessive,**
- **Management isn't showing any capability to control costs, or**
- **The stock has been overly diluted with new share issues.**

Farthing continued, "But, if you can generate a solid, factual case that a turnaround is likely in the near to long term, buying at a low can be very profitable."

Wade placed another overhead.

A STOCK SHORT COURSE:

RULE #1: BE SYSTEMATIC IN MAKING YOUR CHOICES

"There are thousands of companies from which to choose. You don't pick the most likely winners accidentally—witness, again, Warren Buffett. Buffett has only about 10 stocks in his portfolio and he holds them for many years all the while benefiting from capital appreciation, dividends, share splits, etc. You don't want quantity—you want quality."

Overhead:

WATCH FOR:

- **share buybacks**
- **insider buying**
- **serious debt reduction efforts**
- **serious cost cutting efforts**
- **steady earnings growth**
- **innovations and efficiency initiatives**
- **a company that has a respected name and safe niche**

"I hope all of these pluses are obvious. Does anyone want to discuss why these are good things to find in your stock-selection research?"

No hands went up.

"Okay, let's talk for a moment about another good approach."

Overhead:

BUY QUALITY, AND DIVIDENDS ARE NICE

"Investors who don't have the time or inclination to watch the market and keep informed about economic cycles can do well by buying quality stocks that pay regular dividends.

"This approach will see your portfolio grow from modest capital appreciation plus a predictable percentage from dividends. Top-quality companies with established market niches are difficult to knock off and the buy-and-hold strategy can make a lot of sense. And even when the stock price isn't growing, dividend yields ensure your investment is growing."

Overhead:

Examples:

Stock	'87–'88 Price	'94–'95 Price	Dividend (%)
London Insurance	$13.50	$ 27.00	5–6.0
Power Financial	10.00	35.75	3.0+
Rothmans	36.50	100.00	4.0+
Royal Bank	12.82	31.88	4.0+
WIC Western	9.13	15.75	3.5
Xerox	13.00	51.00	3.0

"You can see that holding any of these stocks for these 8 years would have netted an investor pretty decent capital appreciation and also an annual dividend that kept pace with inflation. You can spot stocks such as these in the *Canada Company Handbook* published by Globe Information Services."

Overhead:

LIMIT TRADING—BROKERAGE FEES CAN KILL YOU

"The truth of this point should have been made, at least in part, at the beginning of this evening in the first handout, but just because it's obvious doesn't stop a lot of investors from missing it.

"There's interesting psychology at work in the stock market and a lot of conflicting advice. For example—"

Overhead:

SET A SELL TARGET, SAY 30% ABOVE THE PURCHASE PRICE, AND SELL WHENEVER A STOCK REACHES THIS LEVEL

"There are serious problems with this approach to 'taking profits.' For instance, does this 30-percent gain include brokerage fees? If so, it means your gain is probably only about 25 percent, if you pay 2.5 percent for both the buy and the sell. If it doesn't, you have to wait for the stock to reach a 35-percent gain to cover the brokerage fees.

"Popping in and out of stocks gets very expensive. Many investors spend thousands of dollars in brokers' fees in just a few years."

Overhead:

AUTOMATIC SELLS CAN COST YOU BIG-TIME

"Selling automatically may sound like a good way to lock in profits, but it totally disregards the future potential of a stock. Perhaps a 30-percent gain in price is only the beginning if you've bought a stock in a healthy company in the early stage of a prolonged growth phase.

"Doesn't it make sense to do research to see if the company has the following:"

- **low debt**
- **a safe market niche**
- **insider buying**
- **new products/services on the horizon**
- **share buybacks, and**
- **a program of cost reduction**

"If your research produces 'yes' responses to such questions, it seems ludicrous to sell a stock that could well appreciate many times more than the 30 percent.

"On the surface, resorting to 'automatic pilot' in the stock market may sound like a good rule to force people to take profits and not wait until a stock begins to decline, but 30-percent profits aren't enough over the long haul to cover your inevitable loser stocks. You need what former Fidelity Manager Peter Lynch calls 'the ten baggers'— stocks that rise tenfold in price.

"I should add that Canada is a much more cyclical market than the U.S. We don't have the same size of companies or the sheer number of them, and our market tends to bounce around more because of the constant trading by mutual fund companies and institutional buyers as they all vie for the best quarterly returns to keep their investors.

"So, the ten-baggers aren't as easy to find here but a couple come to mind from recent years: Newbridge Networks, TSE, and Bre-X Minerals, TSE. Newbridge rose from $3.55 per share in 1991 to almost $100 in 1996; Bre-X shot from less than $2 to about $200 in 1996. The Bre-X example means a $5,000 investment would have grown to half a million in one year! It doesn't take too many winners like these to help your net worth. Of course, it's now apparent that Bre-X shareholders also faced a significant downside as the stock plunged again to the $2 range in April 1997.

"Selling strong stocks poses another problem. It means you have sold a company that has demonstrated excellent performance. Now what do you do with your money? Unless you want to sit on the sidelines, you have to find another stock with fundamentals that are just as good as the one you sold. They're out there, but even the best stock pickers lose on about three of every 10 stocks.

"My closing rule harkens back to a time-tested stock market saying: *take profits slowly* and always know why you're taking them."

Overhead:

STOP-LOSS ORDERS: THEY WILL COST YOU, TOO

"Some people favor stop-loss orders. The typical argument is that automatic stop losses force you out of a stock if it declines more than a certain percentage—say 10 to 15 percent. It's true that your loss will be cut on some stocks, but to the 10 to 15 percent loss you have to add broker fees so the loss really becomes more like 14 to 19 percent.

"It makes better investment sense, as far as I'm concerned, to analyze why a company's stock may be falling in price. Given the schizophrenic mood in North American markets of late, even good companies with bright futures can suffer sudden sharp price drops but then recover within a few weeks or months.

"Again, do the necessary research to find out why something is happening to your stock. If, indeed, the company's market position has been eclipsed by an aggressive competitor, or if the company has bought another company and diversified to the point where its real business gets murky, or if its debt rises too high, there's a glut in supply, etc., it may well be time for you to sell.

"The point here is—"

Overhead:

If you buy a company based on careful research, you should sell it based on the same kind of research. Understand the companies you buy, not for the purpose of falling in love with them, but in order to help control your emotions if the market undergoes undulations. Sell when there is a good reason to do so, not just because everybody else is selling. Good companies are good companies.

"People who are attracted to strategies like automatic sells are probably better advised to buy equity mutual funds. Most institutional buyers try to keep up with a company's future prospects, and if they're doing it it's one less thing for you to worry about."

Overhead:

SPEAKING OF MUTUAL FUNDS

"If you don't have the time or inclination to do systematic research before buying and selling stocks, equity mutual funds are probably your best bet. There are some very good equity mutual funds available in Canada that provide consistently good levels of return.

"There are also many good books available that rank mutual funds' performances over a period of many years. Both the *Globe and Mail* and *Financial Post* publish regular mutual-fund supplements on long-term performance.

"The best advice I can give on these funds is to take a careful look at no-load funds. Some of the no-loads perform as well as funds with front or rear loads, and it doesn't make much sense to pay 3 or 4 percent for an investment that another company will provide for nothing, and that will give you comparable returns."

Overhead:

MARKET CYCLES: WHAT'S AHEAD?

"Stock markets in North America have gone up most years this century, with the exception of dramatic and well-publicized declines in 1929 and 1987. Over the past 20 years, however, markets in Canada and the U.S. have risen fairly steadily. Even the decline of 1987 lasted only a few months, and there is support for the premise that they will continue to do so into the next millennium."

Overhead:

REASONS FOR MARKET STRENGTH

- **Inflation seems largely under control.**
- **Interest rates are sufficiently low that investment and building are not discouraged by the high costs of borrowing.**
- **Low interest rates make interest-bearing investments less attractive.**
- **Tens of millions of baby boomers in Canada and the U.S. are scraping together all their spare cash and either investing it themselves or turning it over to mutual-fund managers. These hundreds of billions of dollars each year will continue to pour into the investment markets for at least a decade more.**

"This last point bears closer examination.

"While money is pouring into stock markets right now, this trend could begin to reverse as baby boomers near retirement age and decide to become more conservative with their hard-won nest eggs. It is conceivable there will be an investment shift early in the next millennium if too many millions of baby boomers decide to opt for safety and instruct money managers to switch their funds into interest-bearing instruments such as bonds and GICs.

"In reality, people in the 55 to 65 age range could likely remain in the equity markets with some safety, because these people can expect to live 20 to 30 years more and this is long enough to ride out the market hiccups every few years.

"The big factor in determining stock market performance in 10 to 20 years will hinge on how concerned people are about locking in guaranteed annual incomes. If you have $1 million in RRSP investments and you derive your income largely from stock appreciation and stock dividends, it may get scary to stay in markets that are dipping 15 percent and moving up and down like a roller-coaster. Faced with this scenario, many people may opt for guaranteed returns so they can budget for themselves with some degree of certainty.

"Here's something to ponder: that the very influences that are propelling the sustained '90s bull markets could run out of steam between 2005 and 2010:"

Overhead:

THE MOST SUCCESSFUL STOCK INVESTORS ARE PEOPLE WITH COURAGE, THOSE WHO

- **buy companies that are in disfavor but that have strong fundamentals, and**
- **buy when market conditions look the gloomiest.**

This contrarian approach takes advantage of speculator emotions—buy when the rest of the crowd is running scared (bearish) and sell when they are euphoric (bullish).

Overhead:

BUY BUSINESSES YOU CAN UNDERSTAND

"Anyone watching the North American stock markets in recent years has to be impressed with the tremendous gains many of the high technology stocks have made, particularly those involved with computer technology or the Internet. Very small invest-ments in selected stocks made many people rich. The key word here, however, is 'selected.'

"For every big gainer there were several big losers, and in the early days, when none of the stocks in these sectors had demonstrated records of earnings and revenue growth, picking winners was a crapshoot.

"The stock prices of many of these high-tech stars tended to climb relentlessly for a few weeks, leaving the impression that you can jump on almost any day and realize a 10-percent gain over a week or two. But then if one earnings quarter fell short of expectations, one news report came out noting a competitor gaining an edge, or one rumor popped up of a problem with some part of the technology, investors stampeded for the exits and the $20 stock plummeted $10 in a day.

"The lesson here is that not many people have the expertise to really know what's going on in technology. If you do, this may be your market. If you don't, you're making decisions solely on the basis of what someone else thinks—analysts and publications. History demonstrates again and again that these market prognosticators are wrong as often as they're right."

Overhead:

Point to ponder: Leave stocks alone if you don't understand what drives their prices. Don't be one of those people that more informed investors use to help run a price up through speculative greed. Often the "little guy" is left holding deadbeats because those close to the market watch the feeding frenzy and know enough to dump stocks when they get ridiculously overvalued.

Overhead:

IF YOU DON'T "KNOW" WHAT TO DO, DO NOTHING

"A scenario: equities are in the news and markets in Canada and the U.S. are advancing quickly. Interest rates are stable and relatively low, and there's no hint of inflation. You, however, are sitting with 80 percent of your money in a bond fund that's going nowhere and the prospects don't suggest its performance is going to improve. You say to yourself: 'I've got to get into the stock market.'

"You have $50,000 in your bond fund that you want to put into stocks, so you start scanning publications and talking with your broker trying to get that $50,000 in on the action. Within days you've found six stocks that seem to be popular, all are on analysts' recommended lists, and they give you some market depth in their sector diversity.

"You buy the following, all at market price:

1. **West Fraser Timber**: a forestry company.
2. **Mackenzie Financial**: mutual funds, financial planning.
3. **Abacan Resource Corp.**: a Nigerian oil exploration company.
4. **Power Financial of Canada**: a conglomerate.
5. **Methanex**: a producer of methanol.
6. **Motorola**: a well-established high-tech firm to take advantage of your foreign-content allowance.

"Now you relax, job done.

"You watch your stocks over the next month: three are down markedly, one is up and two are doing nothing. Your $50,000 has dwindled by $5,000, including brokerage fees.

"What happened? All of the companies were included in numerous analysts' buy lists. You did your research, right?

"Well, only partly. You found out what people recommended at a certain point but there were other considerations that could have helped *predict* potential problems. For example:

1. The stock of **West Fraser Timber**, a well-run and well-established company, drops from $37 to $29. In the spring of 1995, could you have seen this coming? Yes, if you'd done your own research and projected out a year.

Specifics: you could have made a reasonably intelligent forecast by considering that:

  a) Canada and the U.S. had been involved in softwood lumber talks for some time and the chance existed for Canada's lumber exports to be cut back to its biggest market—the U.S.;
  b) Consumer confidence was low and new housing starts were down and not expected to recover soon; and
  c) Lumber inventories were high across Canada.

Outlook: The stock recovered, but it took almost two years to hit $45.

  2. **Mackenzie Financial:** Stock rose from $11.75 to $19.45 in 1996. Long-term prospects are good, but upside potential is not expected to duplicate '96 performance.

Outlook: Wait and see. No big losses are likely with the continued influx of money into savings plans, returns likely to be in the 15–20 percent range.

  3. **Abacan Resource Corp.:** Serious political turmoil has threatened Nigeria for some time. The military stages a coup within weeks of your buy. Your $4 stock drops to $2.90 and then fluctuates wildly for several months. At the low end you're down more than 25 percent on your investment.

Specifics: The political uncertainty was foreseeable. Military coups often generate talk of trade boycotts by "democratic" nations. Oil was in high supply and talks were continuing to let Iraq start pumping oil into the world marketplace again. In addition, some of Abacan's price is based on built-in speculative optimism about future production.

Outlook: The outlook may be good if all the influences cited are alleviated and future production reaches predicted levels—at the costs budgeted. This is a speculative stock that could do well over the long term, but that could also "tank" if things don't go well. The stock fluctuated widely through the spring, summer, and fall of 1996, yet exceeded $15 by January 1997. For those who bought stock at $2 it's a seven-bagger. The question became, 'Do I hold on and wait for even better gains, or sell and wait for other dips, or look for an entirely different stock?' At press time the correct answer was still unknown.

4. **Power Financial:** Large conglomerate, highly recommended by a variety of analysts. Stock not doing much of anything, trades up and down only a couple of dollars in the $30 range for months in 1996, then breaks out in the summer and fall to rise $20 per share.

Outlook: A "conservative" stock that wasn't projected to produce a 60-percent gain so soon or so quickly. The industry is still poised to do well and there is no 'bad news' suggesting a negative downturn. Downside risk seems minimal. The stock may do well over next several years.

5. **Methanex:** Managed to buy at $9 at a "down dip." Shortly afterward, global methanol inventories began to show signs of running down. A well-run company that has a good ratio between rapidly growing revenues and price/earnings (P/E). Investment gains 18 percent in a few weeks.

Specifics: Shrinking inventories, a decline in price to a 4-year low, a P/E in the range of 7, and revenues that showed no signs of letting up.

Outlook: The stock hit a historical high of $24.50 in 1994, so there is considerable potential upside to net a 100-percent return. Still sells well below the historical high.

6. **Motorola:** Analysts recommend a buy when the stock dips to the mid-$50s US from a high of more than $80 in 1995. The fourth-quarter earnings report for 1995 is slightly below market expectations and the stock drops to $47 over a two-week period. It recovers a bit, then fluctuates mostly in the mid-$50s for months.

Specifics: Motorola's reduced earnings were predictable given its exposure to the increasingly competitive cellular telephone market. The company even admitted in its own news releases that maintaining profits at historical levels would be difficult through the late 1990s.

Outlook: The stock will likely recover, but it could take several years to break even and maybe longer to net a decent return.

"These scenarios are all factual. An investor willing to do some 'personal' research could have made some educated guesses about possible market directions for these stocks. No one will be right all the time, but investors could have found out fairly easily those hints of the bad news that ultimately drove prices down."
  Overhead:

THE LESSON:

Stocks aren't emotional and neither should their owners be. Do the best environmental scan you can, taking into consideration

- **Position within sector**
- **Inventory surpluses or shortages**

- **Political uncertainties**
- **Competitive advantage or disadvantage**
- **Consistent revenue and earnings growth**
- **Good value (such as growth to P/E ratio)**
- **How much of the stock price is speculation?**
- **Stock at historical high, low, middle? Why?**
- **Where is the stock in the cycle? (such as forestry)**
- **Can you get big gains from conservative growers?**

"Asking these questions and taking the time to get the answers will help you make much more informed decisions. Only a fraction of investors take the time to do such research. Maybe this is *why* the others think the stock market is a crapshoot!"

Overhead:

PLACE "BELOW MARKET" OFFERS

"Impatient investors, and those who just don't know any better, often buy a stock at 'market' price. This means you place an order with a broker and pay whatever the asking price is at the time your broker places the order. Often, though, placing an order a bit below the market price will still get you the stock, particularly if the sellers start to get impatient.

"For example, there's a block of stocks offered at $19.50 and the block has been sitting around for some time. Unless you're after a stock that seems to know no direction but up, there's no harm in placing your bid at $19.10, or $19.25, or whatever is reasonable. You will often get the stock within a day or two. You're saving only pennies, but pennies per stock add up and often pay your brokerage fees."

Overhead:

WATCH A STOCK, CAPITALIZE ON DIPS

"Most stocks move up and down across a range every few days. Often investors, once they've decided to buy a stock, do so at market prices. This is a good strategy for a stock that seems certain of going up and not down, but you can often buy a stock a dollar or two cheaper if you're just a little patient.

"With stocks that aren't doing anything dramatic either way, you can afford to watch for temporary 'dips' in price. Keep in touch with your broker and, keep track of market prices so you can try to capitalize on that small dip. This can also save you money.

"For example, a stock trading at $20 will cost you $20.50, assuming you pay a 2.5-percent brokerage fee. Watch the stock until it dips to $19.50 and you can buy it for $20. Then you'll be ahead of the entire brokerage fee."

Overhead:

CALL A COMPANY'S INVESTOR RELATIONS DEPARTMENT

"Most people are reluctant to do this, yet most people in investor relations departments are happy to talk with even small investors. The types of information you get varies, and it depends, of course, on the quality of your questions and conversation. You can probe why a stock is moving in a certain direction, discuss the company's debt reduction, stock buybacks, efficiencies, and any plans for new products or services that have just become public knowledge.

"Investor relations staff are often quite forthcoming in what they'll tell you. It's one more bit of information gathering you can do in 10 minutes for the price of a telephone call."

Overhead:

MINIMUM STOCK RESEARCH

"Many books advise stock investors on how to make their investment decisions. The problem with many of them is they're too complicated. Improving the way you select stocks need not be difficult to understand, and you don't have to take a securities course. You can do the job with no more than this—"
Overhead:

1. Take a subscription to the *Globe and Mail* for its *Report on Business* section.
2. Buy the *Globe's Canada Company Handbook*, which is published every summer.
3. Find a broker willing to get you the latest information on quarterly earnings and other financial data companies report routinely.

"For about $240 per year, the *Globe and Mail* will keep you current about market news, daily stock prices, company profiles, annual reports, and news about insider buying and selling, and more.
"For about $70 per year, you get the *Canada Company Handbook*, which gives you a lot of the historical information you need:

- stock price changes for numerous consecutive years
- dividend yields
- price/earnings ratios
- sales per share
- cash flow per share
- book value per share
- number of shares outstanding
- total revenue

- debt/equity ratio
- return on capital
- profit/revenue growth
- cash, assets, liabilities
- company descriptions, synopses, and outlooks.

"The *Handbook* is published every summer, so it isn't current for long, but most brokers bring data up to date quickly. With this book and your broker you can keep up-to-date quickly and cheaply."
  Overhead:

WHAT YOU'RE LOOKING FOR: SPECIFICS ABOUT STOCK PICKING

"A simple 'criteria-driven' system can help you develop a habit of screening stocks before making your buy decisions.
  "Let me hand out some more papers that detail the type of research I propose."

STOCK RESEARCH

Buy one of the books or publications available to the general public (such as the *Globe* Information Services' *Canada Company Handbook*). You can obtain all of the following information easily, but only a fraction of investors takes the time and trouble to assemble it. You should know about:

1. Stock price fluctuations over long periods of time: a) 60 months; b) 60 weeks. Does the stock price show a steady upward march, or the peaks and valleys of a cyclical or uneven performer?
2. Earnings per share per quarter and per year for the past 5 years. Look for consistent growth, preferably 10 percent or

---

better per year. Earnings deceleration over successive quarters can be a sign of trouble.

3. Revenue growth per quarter and per year for the past 5 years. Again, revenue should show consistent growth.

4. Annual profit growth. This should also show growth over a prolonged period.

5. The price/earnings ratio (P/E ratio) relative to the industry. P/E ratio and growth percentages should be about equal, but it's a good sign if the growth percentage is higher.

6. Dividends paid for past 5 years. Good if dividend paid regularly and growing. Not all stocks pay dividends, and dividends are not necessary if other factors remain positive.

7. Sales per share should show improvement over a multi-year period.

8. Cash flow should be rising.

9. Book value per share. An increase shows the company's worth is growing with its revenues.

10. Insider buying in past year? Insider buying is a good sign. "Insiders" know the company, and their faith is often well-placed. Various publications will report this information.

11. Are institutions buying the stock? Information about institutional positions are available in publications or from your broker. Buying by institutions can be a good sign, but small investors can get caught in downslides if those same institutions decide to dump millions of shares onto the market. For this reason, excessive institutional positions can make a stock subject to sudden fluctuation.

12. Any recent debt paydowns? A company that shows concern for reducing its debt suggests wise management. Debt paydowns also improve a company's value.

13. Does the company buy back its own shares? Companies that buy their own shares are usually confident of their future

prospects. Also, shares removed from the marketplace reduce share dilution.

14. New products, services, technological/efficiency advancements, or expansions on the horizon? These can all be good signs if management has done its homework and the new directions don't seem likely to turn sour, fracture the company's focus, or incur excessive debt. The marketplace will punish a stock if its "newness" is perceived as having more downsides than upsides.

15. Are the company's assets significantly greater than its liabilities? Companies with healthy asset-to-debt ratios have higher "share-price floors," the level below which a share price is not likely to fall.

16. Compare growth related to earnings and dividends: Find the long-term growth rate (e.g., 12%), add dividend yield (e.g., 3%). Divide by P/E ratio (e.g., 10, so $12 + 3 \div 10 = 1.5$). Less than 1 is poor, 1.5 is okay; but 2 or better is good. A company with 15% growth, a 3% dividend yield, and a P/E ratio of 6 would be a 3 (great).

17. **Important**: Determine as best you can the prospects for future earnings and profit growth. Since this is "future watch," it is not possible to be 100-percent accurate. By watching companies carefully for a period of time, however, by determining whether they are "cutting edge," and by assembling information about the growth prospects in the particular industry, you can get a better picture of the probable direction of the company and the industry. Share prices often fluctuate, up and down, with the release of quarterly earnings reports, so it is sometimes good strategy to wait for the report, get the information as quickly as possible and decide to buy or not once you know the latest information. Often a share will continue to rise in price for several days after release of a positive quarterly report.

Conversely, share price will often sink rapidly with release of what the market considers a "bad" report. Better to get on while the price is on the rise rather than buying a week before only to see your stock driven down by $5 a share. You still may want to buy, if all your research shows the company to be a good prospect, but buy at the lower price after the market has kneejerked.

18. Investigate initial public offerings (IPOs) early. While IPOs don't have a track record and can be speculative in the early stages they are also companies to watch. Often you can see a trend after a year or so and take advantage of a stock's appreciation in the early years when the company grows quickly. Here again, be patient; some stocks rise quickly on speculation more than reality. In the stock market the best predictor of future performance is past performance—you can afford to wait if the company really has a future.

19. Watch specific industries, and stocks within those industries, that are likely, given economic, demographic trends, etc. to realize significant growth in the coming years. This necessitates scanning the future horizon for opportunities. For example, funeral home companies have done very well in recent years, but there may be a period of decline over the years when the current population of elderly die, and the time when baby boomers reach mortality limits. Baby boomers began turning 50 in 1996, so the "big wave" of boomer deaths isn't likely to begin until about 2021–2026 (75–80 years of age). A company, such as the Loewen Group, may be a "strong buy" about 2019 and then expect a long hold as revenues turn up for the next 20 years.

And obviously before the boomers start to actually die, they are going to require numerous health-related products and services—anticipating what they'll need a few years before the peak demand hits could reveal companies that are well positioned for dramatic future growth.

GENERAL INDICATORS

1. *P/E ratios on the low end for the particular industry.* Sometimes good companies will have high P/Es and can sustain the price. Your research can help you judge, but all things being equal the company with the lower P/E may have more room for appreciation.
2. *A steady Bank of Canada rate below 8 percent.* When the rate rises above 8 percent, and especially above 10 percent, markets get very nervous about the high costs associated with corporate borrowing. This can be a time to divest yourself of most stocks and wait for higher interest rates to make bonds attractive. Then, wait for a return to lower rates and take your "no-risk" 10%-bond returns until they arrive and the stock market revives.
3. *Consumer confidence.* Low consumer confidence does not bode well for some sectors of the market (the retail, automotive, and housing sectors).
4. *Where are other stocks in same industry going?* Is your company a leader or a laggard?
5. *Watch the Canadian dollar.* A lower dollar is good for exports and the companies that rely on exports for their revenue.
6. *Watch inflation.* Any sign of a significant resurgence of inflation can drive the markets down quickly. These can be times to buy if you are a long-term, patient investor. Just don't jump in too quickly, wait for signs the correction is over, but you don't have to buy at the absolute bottom—you may miss it.
7. *What is the Federal Reserve doing in the U.S.?* Given our trade interdependence now, Canada's markets rise and fall in lockstep with the U.S. over the long term.

A Good Rule of Thumb

"There's an even easier way to keep your finger on the economic pulse, and despite its apparent simplicity it's worked pretty well over the past few decades.

"All this approach requires is that you watch the Bank of Canada rate. When the rate is below 8 percent, you should have your investments in equities, in either individual stocks or equity mutual funds. When the rate hits 8 percent, switch into money-market instruments or a money-market mutual fund until you see which way the interest rates are headed.

"If rates continue to rise, sit quietly in the money market until prices seem to have peaked, then move into bonds or bond mutual funds. Once the rates start to come down again, and they always do, you'll profit hugely on each percentage point drop.

"If rates move back below 8 percent and it's apparent the general trend is toward sustained lower rates, move back into equities.

"This strategy is logical, not complicated. When money for borrowing is cheap, business and the stock market do well; when the cost of borrowing rises, they don't. If you move with the direction of the Bank of Canada rate and use money markets as a safe haven while you analyze where things are going, you can do well over the long run.

"Now, here are some economic and stock analysis worksheets that offer the investor a systematic approach to selecting stocks. Following these steps will not guarantee that all your stocks will be winners. They will ensure that you choose those stocks on the basis of factual information rather than gut instinct or rumors.

"Anyone can easily gather all the information required to assemble a stock profile. You don't have to have a degree in business to understand the process. Try it."

STOCK APPROACHES FOR "AN EDGE" (SAFE)

Stock Name: _____

Date: _____

Current Price: _____

General Economic Indicators:

	Pos	Neut	Neg
1. Bank of Canada rate?	____	____	____
a) Bank of Canada rate's direction?	____	____	____
2. U.S. Federal Reserve rate?	____	____	____
a) Federal Reserve rate direction?	____	____	____
3. Canadian dollar's level: Direction?	____	____	____
4. Consumer confidence direction?	____	____	____
5. Canadian dollar considered low?	____	____	____
6. Inflation under control?	____	____	____

(Note: Interest rates below 8% are desired, and an increase/decrease of more than ½% can signal sudden market reversals and "buy/sells."

Inflation should be under control and the Canadian dollar stable, preferably below 80 cents (U.S.) if the industry you're considering depends on exports.)

Specific Stock Analysis:

	Pos	Neut	Neg
1. P/E ratio?	____	____	____
(At low end of industry?)			
2. Most recent quarter EPS up 10%+	____	____	____
Previous 1/4s ____ ____ ____			
3. Steady earnings increase over 2+ years?	____	____	____
1994 ____ 1995 ____ 1996 ____			
4. Revenue, profit, cash-flow growth?	____	____	____
1994 ____ 1995 ____ 1996 ____			
5. New products, management, direction?	____	____	____

Specific Stock Analysis:

	Pos	Neut	Neg
6. Direction of stocks in the same industry?	____	____	____
7. Insider buying/selling taking place?	____	____	____
8. Has the stock begun a discernible upward move?	____	____	____
9. Stock's behavior in relation to the rest of market?	____	____	____

10. Rationale for believing earnings growth will continue:

_____

_____

(Note: Positive responses are critical to almost all questions; no insider selling trend should be evident. Negatives suggests caution—possible "wait and see.")

Wade Farthing continued.

"I'm about done for tonight," he said, "but I do want to leave you with ideas about stocks that you might start watching to see if they demonstrate some of the traits we've touched on. All of these companies use technology, and there will undoubtedly be some big gainers in the group if you're comfortable with high tech. At any rate, thank you for listening to me tonight and thank you for coming."

Another sheet was passed around and the crowd slowly drifted out.

As we strolled back to the cottage I remarked to Gordon that Wade Farthing had really motivated me to learn more about the stock market and how the overall economy works.

"That's great," he said. "Boning up on your knowledge about the market and economy can be both challenging and interesting."

"So what do you think is the best way to start? I guess I could enroll in a night course at one of the universities to get up to speed."

"Yes, you could," he answered, "but I'd be awfully careful about first checking out the qualifications of the professors or instructors."

"Why, don't you have much confidence in our academics?"

"Quite honestly, no," he said. "From experience I've come to the conclusion that too many of our educators, and especially those in business and economics faculties, haven't proven they can function successfully in the real business world. A lot of knowledge coupled with little experience often conceals insecurity and a confused ego. What good is it to be highly educated but lack worldly wisdom?

"Cosmo has a good perspective on this. What is it he says? 'Intellectuals love to focus on complexity and theoretical mental rigor. Intellectually they soar high and dive deep—but they seldom pay cash.'"

I read Wade Farthing's stock trends sheet when we got back to the cottage and was intrigued by some of the possibilities. I also thought I might skip the university course.

STOCKS AND TRENDS TO WATCH

Ballard Power: A research and development firm creating fuel cells for homes and vehicles that run on oxygen, hydrogen, or methane. Fuel cells are pollution-free and generate only heat and distilled water as byproducts. Initial tests are very promising. Major automotive companies worldwide have signed contracts with Ballard to get in on the R&D (research and development). The stock doubled from about $8 in spring 1995 to more than $39 in 1996. With sales in the billions of dollars projected early in the next millennium, stock-price appreciation is promising if the company keeps a leading edge in the field, meets progress targets, and controls costs.

Philip Environmental: Specializes in environmental cleanup and disposal of industrial waste products—possibly a high-growth field in coming years. Stock has been gaining rapidly and is worth more research and watching.

Footmax: A new idea that will use computers in shoe stores to analyze foot problems and manufacture inserts to correct the problems identified "on the spot." This could be a real growth company if the technology works well and the footwear chains pick it up.

Motorola: A leader in the field of personal communication devices that don't require base sets and wires. Has also forged an alliance with Apple Computer. Volatile stock in 1996 but strong earnings growth could see the stock reach all-time highs once again.

Home Direct Movie Operations: Video stores are likely to go the way of the dinosaurs in the next few years. Watch those companies able to offer fiber-optic movies directly to homes. When they hit the market, watch for rising stars with strong fundamentals—avoid getting caught up in hype—it will probably pay to watch for a while until the real leaders emerge.

The first Internet Cafe Franchise: None exist yet, but they will. Again, watch the fundamentals and don't get caught up in emotion.

Companies that make and input information and images on CDs: Technology now permits companies to fit 1,000 books on a single CD. Soon it will be possible to accommodate 10,000 books. CD-ROM bookstores will emerge.

Companies that manufacture computers with the ergonomics of a book: People like to curl up instead of sitting erect at a computer. The first companies to produce ergonomically friendly "book computers" will secure a market niche, at least briefly, until competitors improve the concept.

Virtual-reality equipment: This technology features body suits with tactile sensors that enable you to transmit touch via long distance—safe sex in the privacy of your home, plus many other applications not even thought of yet.

(Note: Neither the author nor the publisher is recommending that readers buy any of the stocks mentioned in this book. Names and specific examples are provided for demonstration purposes only. Conditions change and investors should conduct their own, more current research before deciding to purchase any stocks.)

Home's not merely four square walls,
Though with pictures hung and gilded;
Home is where affection calls,
Filled with shrines the Heart has builded.

— Charles Swain

CHAPTER 8

Your Principal Residence: Mining the Silver Lining

Chapter Goal: To demonstrate alternative uses of assets gained from selling the principal residence at retirement and securing less expensive accommodation.

DAY 3, Late Evening

By nine o'clock the evening sun had sunk below the horizon, still casting a warm golden glow over the mountaintops to the east. Gordon and I sat on the patio, cold drinks in hand, chairs tilted back and heels resting on an intricate lodge pole railing created from the twisted treasures Gordon and Sara had found in their driftwood hunts.

Insects flew erratic zigzags over the water's surface. Every minute or so a rising trout splashed through the smooth surface to catch its supper. The silence was warm, close, and comfortable. I could easily imagine myself being very happy in a spot like this in a few years' time.

Gordon broke the silence.

"So, what do you think of The Last Resort, now that you've had a bit of time to see how things work?"

"What's to think? It's beautiful. When I first arrived I wondered how you could uproot yourselves from Toronto and leave friends and family, but the longer I'm here the more removed I feel from Vancouver! I guess it wasn't too difficult a transition?"

"Not really. To be honest, we didn't know at first how special this place would become. As you say, whenever we lived in Canada we stayed in and around Toronto, so we did feel a bit apprehensive about leaving everything there to 'go west.' Then we started listing the things we considered negative about retirement in Toronto that we would want to change:

- The old house was quite large—more than 2,000 square feet for just the two of us.
- Stairs going up and stairs going down. There'll likely come a time when stairs won't be a good idea or even possible for one or both of us.
- The lot was of a typical size for a city, 60 feet by 120 feet, but there were lots of flower beds and lawn, a really finicky piece of property that demanded constant attention and care. It devoured half our weekends from spring to fall.
- We had a lot of capital invested in that property.
- The highway was only a quarter mile away. Even though we lived on a side street there was the constant kkkkkkkkkkk of white noise around us.
- Crime is on the rise in the area. You certainly didn't feel safe leaving your doors unlocked at any time of day. I didn't say much to Sara, but I was always worried when she chose to walk to the mall a half mile away. Going out walking late at night is out of the question for a woman in most big cities these days. Who needs that kind of stress?

"Thinking about our answers to these kinds of questions made the decision a lot easier. It took us only a few weeks to realize we'd made the right move. We believe now that the people who take the time to come and visit us are our real friends. And, hell, we've banked enough money from changing our lifestyle to be able to afford to fly our relatives out here every couple of years."

I had to ask. "You really found it that much of a saving? To look at the cottage I can't imagine you saved much."

"Oh, sure we did! By keeping the house in Toronto and maintaining our principal residence status, we did quite well. When we sold the house for about $226,000, we netted $214,567 after real estate commissions, GST on that real estate commission, and some small vendor closing costs.*

"With about $92,000 it took to build the cottage, plus an additional $6,000 for appliances and legal fees, we still managed to bank $116,567.

"At age 65, we made the assumption this money should be 'run down' over a 20-year period. Now, this money, through a combination of principal and interest, contributes about $10,000 a year to our income, assuming a constant rate of interest at 6 percent per year. I have a 20-year table of projections I can show you."

He returned a moment later with yet another sheet of paper. "This should be interesting for you because I believe it reflects dollar sums that would parallel those of many people leaving higher priced urban areas for less expensive smaller towns and cities. There's no mystery to getting access to the money—it's just another of those choices people should consider before they retire. Have a look. You'll see how I arrived at the $10,000 a year in extra income by using interest and principal draw-down."

---

* Commission calculation is 6 percent on the first $100,000, 3 percent on the balance and 7 percent GST on the total.

HOUSE SALE: INTEREST AND PRINCIPAL PROJECTIONS

Year	Capital	Interest on Capital	Principal Draw-Down for Year	Income for Year
1996	$116,567	$6,994	$3,000	$ 9,994
1997	113,567	6,814	3,000	9,814
1998	110,567	6,634	3,000	9,634
1999	107,567	6,454	4,000	10,454
2000	103,567	6,214	4,000	10,214
2001	99,567	5,974	4,000	9,974
2002	95,567	5,734	4,000	9,734
2003	91,567	5,494	4,500	9,994
2004	87,067	5,224	4,500	9,724
2005	82,567	4,954	5,000	9,954
2006	77,567	4,654	6,000	10,654
2007	71,567	4,294	6,000	10,294
2008	65,567	3,934	7,000	10,934
2009	58,567	3,514	7,000	10,514
2010	51,567	3,094	7,000	10,094
2011	44,567	2,674	8,000	10,674
2012	36,567	2,194	8,000	10,194
2013	28,567	1,714	9,000	10,714
2014	19,567	1,174	9,000	10,174
2015	10,567	634	11,201	11,201
TOTAL		**$88,370**	**$117,201**	**$204,937**

After I'd scanned the figures, Gordon went on.

"Although inflation will gradually·erode the value of our $10,000 or so in income per year, we expect our travel and some other major activity expenses will decline, so our financial needs will be reduced accordingly.

"We've had people say; 'Well, $10,000 a year in extra income isn't that great.' Our answer is, maybe not, but the money we earn from the surplus house capital doesn't give the whole picture. We also save significantly compared to what we had to spend to maintain the older house. Specifically:

Taxes in Toronto	$4,300 per year
Utilities in Toronto	$2,100 per year
Total costs in Toronto	$6,400 per year
Taxes now	$2,000 per year
Utilities now	$1,200 per year
Total costs now per year	$3,200 per year
Savings (difference)	**$3,200 per year**

"Spread that annual saving over 20 years and we're another $64,000 better off. And this doesn't take into account the money we would have had to spend to maintain the Toronto house compared to this new one, which really shouldn't need much in the way of repairs or replacements for at least 20 years.

"The way we see it, we're $268,937 ahead if we include freed-up capital, interest on that capital, plus savings in taxes and utilities—and we haven't sacrificed a thing. In fact, we think we're much happier here than we would have been in Toronto. And we've got that extra $13,000 a year to enjoy—that's a pretty nice two-month holiday every January and February!

"I should also add," he went on, "that we might be able to do better than a 6-percent return on our house capital account, but we've done our projections and have enough to support precisely the way we want to live. So, why take any chances to try for the extra percentage points you *might* get from equity investments?"

"We know from doing your projections that you would benefit

even more from the sale of your city residence than we did," said Gordon.

I had to admit getting an extra quarter-million dollars over the retirement years provided a pretty good kick to available resources. Selling our place in Vancouver in a few years was something I'd have to discuss with Lorraine.

"The $150,000 that will let you live for almost three years without touching your RRSP/RRIF and the tax-sheltered compounding they'll do will give you a lot of financial flexibility. And I'm willing to bet your real estate taxes in the Lower Mainland are going to become pretty rude over the next 20 years. Just $1,000 a year saved in taxes and another $1,000 in utilities would add another $40,000 to your retirement nest egg from the ages 65 to 85! So, you'd get almost three years of income, plus all the other savings, *plus* let your other RRSPs compound in a sheltered place. I'll bet we're talking about half a million extra dollars—not small potatoes even in two to three decades."

I sipped my drink thoughtfully.

"I know Lorraine likes our house, but neither of us has looked at what it could do for our retirement income and security. I don't think she likes it to the tune of half a million dollars."

"Well, assuming you do agree to sell in the city and consider the retirement village concept, let's spend some time talking about some things you should know about *that* idea."

Oh, to have a little house!
To own the hearth and stool and all!

— Padraic Colum

CHAPTER 9

Your Last Resort

Chapter Goal: To provide tips on setting up a "last resort," how to save money during construction, the range of service options, and related information.

DAY 3, Late Evening

THE RETIREMENT VILLAGE CONCEPT

"I guess this is as good a time as any to fill you in on how The Last Resort was started and what we had to do to take it from idea to reality.

"First, we had to find people who genuinely valued a pleasant and relaxed living environment. This wasn't difficult.

"One of the most important things in life is having a good house," said Gordon. "I suspect it's something instinctive. Consider what many people do and how they spend their time and money when they don't have quality accommodation that makes them feel secure and comfortable. They charge around frenetically and spend all kinds of money on gadgets, holidays, and nonstop socializing in pursuit of 'something.' I think that something is what you have when you have a place you enjoy where you can sit and contemplate your life and the world.

"And I'm not talking about having just any old house. I

227

believe a house has to be something more than functional. It should reflect the personality and lifestyles of its owners."

MAKING IMPORTANT DECISIONS

"I think deciding where to live in retirement is one of the most important decisions people make. Frequently the decision is partly made for them according to two key considerations: health and money. If you have good health and sufficient money, the decision is much easier—you can do whatever you want. If, however, you lack the health or the money, you have to make harder choices.

In setting up the village and in working out the strategic plan we adopted a slogan: "Observe always: reciprocity, cooperation, and mutuality." Here're the criteria we all used when we were discussing the Resort concept:"

1. Is your health, and that of your spouse (if you have one), good enough for you to live independently?
2. In terms of money alone, can you afford to live the rest of your life (lives) in your current home?
3. Do you feel you must live in a home that is completely detached?
4. How much privacy do you require?
5. How satisfied are you with the following in your current location:

- climate,
- available transportation,
- pollution/allergens,
- crime,
- security,
- floor plan (as your physical abilities decline),
- your residence's maintenance demands,

- taxes, utilities, cost of living,
- social opportunities,
- access to outlets for your hobbies and interests,
- proximity to family and friends,
- shopping,
- professional services (legal, health, other), and
- traffic congestion.

"One of the factors that made this area so appealing was its proximity to golf courses, skiing, hiking, and the water. It's a pristine area that should stay this way for many years to come."

LIVING OPTIONS

"Once you begin to look at retirement accommodation seriously you'll realize there's a host of possibilities to suit almost every taste and desire. For example, consider the following:

- a private home, apartment, condo, or mobile home,
- a retirement community,
- low-income rental or co-op housing,
- shared living,
- boarding homes,
- adult family homes,
- nursing homes, or
- intentional communities.

"Perhaps the only one of these that requires elaboration is intentional communities. These are housing alternatives arranged by people who come together in groups around shared value systems or individual preferences. For example, a particular religion could be the focal point, or artistic or creative expression— in other words, people with similar interests and skills that share them for the benefit of all."

A Word about Manufactured Home Retirement Villages

"Let me say at the outset that there are options other than the one we chose. For older people who can't afford traditional construction, manufactured or mobile homes still permit them many of the benefits of independent living at a lower cost. There are hundreds of trailer courts in California and Arizona full of trailers, and they offer all the services we've covered so far. The only difference is the construction methods used for the structures in which these residents live."

Retirement Communities

"Generally," Gordon continued, "retirement communities are an option for elderly people in good health and with enough money to cover all anticipated expenses.

"These communities come in all shapes and sizes. Some are just a collection of dwellings with few services. Others are huge developments offering recreation complexes, swimming pools, numerous golf courses, that sort of thing. One such community, Sun City, Arizona (population 45,000+), has grown so large that complete infrastructures have sprung up just to serve its aging residents: shopping malls, hospitals, cultural groups, museum, banks, churches.

"These mega-developments are the exception, though. Most retirement communities are more modest. The relatively small developments can offer several levels of independence depending on their residents' needs. Consider some of the categories that can be combined in a single development based on various health and financial situations:

- Independent private ownership: Residents own their homes and take care of their own affairs entirely.
- Independent rental: Residents pay a monthly fee for their accommodation and property maintenance.
- Endowment: For an initial investment and usually a monthly fee, and under a contractual agreement,

residents are 'guaranteed' lifelong care suited to their specific needs: food, skilled health care, house-keeping, laundry, activities.

- Assisted living: Help is provided, usually on a fee-for-service basis, for whatever needs people have—meals, dressing, bathing, laundry, housekeeping, monitoring medications, property maintenance."

I hmphed. "The concept sounds logical, but my dealings with people in the business world have made me skeptical about the willingness of different people to all pull in the same direction at once, and to keep pulling in that direction.

"It would be pretty complicated to get a fairly large group of people to agree on a site and the other compromises that have to be made to actually create and run a retirement village."

"Yes," said Gordon, "it isn't a snap, but if you have a plan, you can do it. Let me show you the one we used."

Organizational Steps

"Only four people conceptualized the initial idea. It fell to them to network with friends and associates to see if they could inter-est the number of people they knew they would need to pull the project together.

"Getting enough interested people wasn't difficult at all, particularly once they put the plan on paper and had something to show people. That made the benefits clear. The number of individuals who were interested and tentatively committed grew to 10 within two months. Sara and I got involved at that stage. We became part of the core group that undertook to do the preliminary research. This plan details what we did, given our proximity to the lake, but a similar approach could be used anywhere. Have a look at the process I've assembled for people interested in exploring the concept themselves."

He passed me another sheet of paper.

Development Steps

1. Research regional district bylaws regarding population density regulations, water and sewer requirements, and the availability of suitable pieces of land, preferably a minimum of 10 acres on the lake and relatively flat.
2. Set preliminary goals and principles. Participants should know from the outset if, for example, the village is to be a 'community of people who can also be friends,' or whether the community will be more private, with little planned social interaction. Setting such goals is important because they influence all future policies and physical design.

"Once you can find suitable land and you can meet local zoning and water and sewer requirements, the project can move to the next stage:

---

3. Obtain financial commitments, and refundable deposits, from the required number of interested and tentatively committed parties.
4. Obtain the land: find an appropriate piece of property and make an offer to purchase it contingent on your obtaining the necessary government approvals for the number of building sites you wish. (In the case of The Last Resort we planned for 20 individual one-third-acre lots.) Consider as well the residents' need for common areas and determine whether those people who live adjacent to the property accept the village concept.
5. Contract for a preliminary architect's plan.
6. Use the financial commitments and architectural drawings you've obtained to date to secure any additional commitments

---

you need to fill the village or at least however many people you need to proceed.

7. Obtain official regional district approvals for the development. The purchase contingencies will be removed once it is clear the project will receive the necessary government approvals.

8. With the finances committed and the land purchased, you give building contractors the architect's plans and receive bids for the common buildings and owner cottages.

9. Begin construction.

Deciding on the Atmosphere

"When setting up the resort, we had a choice. We could opt for a condominium setting or individual dwellings. We chose the latter because everyone in The Resort preferred detached houses. No one wanted to be cooped up in a beehive-style home!

"As you see, the setting is natural. We've left as many trees as possible and disturbed the natural setting very little. This gives a park-like feel and also means less fiddling with totally manicured spaces. We each have our own space, and it's up to us to look after what we have. The common areas are left as virgin as possible because we like it that way. Of course this also means less maintenance. Our part-time groundskeeper can look after those areas easily.

"I know of few people who would say apartment buildings or condos are beautiful, or that they provide a sense of peace and ease. Yet everyone who visits The Resort appreciates what we have here.

"You'll also notice that the driveways and entrance roads run down the sides of the property. This was done deliberately to preserve the property's park-like feeling. The center of the land is devoted to buildings and amenities for people, not vehicles.

Crafting a Design

"The architects created a plan that offered us the best subdivision of the property possible to permit construction of the 20 cottages. Each sits on a lot of about one-third of an acre. Building sites were laid out to provide privacy and easy access to common open spaces at the same time. Flagstone paths wind through the green common area in the center.

"We also found easy agreement that cottage exteriors should not clash with each other or with the forest setting. So we established rules regarding the heights, sizes, styles, and exterior building materials. Common buildings mirrored these exterior policies, too.

"All of us who live here are also very conscious of environmental concerns. We guard the physical health and integrity of The Resort very jealously. We operate village recycling and compost centers to minimize our waste and we use everything that can be composted in our gardens.

"Another area where the architects were a great help was in planning interiors suitable for older people. They made sure everyone thought about the devices that may come into our lives at some point—things like wheelchairs. To accommodate those contraptions you need three-foot wide doors, wide corridors, no stairs and other troublesome thresholds, adequate space to turn in all rooms and easy access everywhere.

"Kitchens and baths sport special equipment, like pull-out boards and handrails in key locations. You'll also notice that all the kitchen and bath cabinets are pull-out drawers, not swing doors that mean you have to get down on your hands and knees to see what's inside of the lower shelves. We don't need them now, but who knows what will happen in 20 years? I should add that we find them so much more user-friendly right now that we wonder why we didn't always have them!"

Management

"Management responsibility is shared among our residents," he said. "Owners decide on rules and policies to govern The Resort and ensure that new owners understand and are willing to conform to these criteria.

"We have an elected board that changes annually. Holding a position on it isn't onerous. Most of its work involves book-keeping and organizational and secretarial tasks. All major decisions are made by vote by all owners. Monthly board meetings are held to take care of any details, or whenever it's necessary to get the entire village's input or votes.

"The board strikes subcommittees as needed. Its members may need help handling any number of tasks: coordinating events, collecting fees, and managing treasury matters, financial and legal.

"In answer to your concern about disagreements, I'm happy to say that there have been very few of these. In large part I think this is because we try to respect the rights of individual owners to deal with their own properties as they see fit. Whatever affects common areas is decided democratically, so we've had very few problems that we couldn't resolve by consensus."

Saving Money in Construction

"Because we were looking at building 20 cottages, plus several common buildings and associated improvements, we were able to extract some healthy discounts from our contractors. We needed a lot of cooperation and consultation among ourselves at the building stage so we could take advantage of economies of scale— bulk purchases of lumber, concrete work, and other building materials, and multiple purchases of things like appliances, heating systems, windows, hardware and equipment, and so on.

"Obviously, we could have built the cottages more inexpensively if we'd all been willing to have houses that were the same, or at least very similar. We discussed this but decided it wasn't for us. Everyone here has decidedly individual tastes. Obviously, we didn't save as much as some developments do, but then we didn't want conformity just to save money. We wanted homes we would be comfortable with."

Money-Saving Specifics

"We learned some really valuable lessons about building costs along the way. Unfortunately, we probably won't ever get to use this knowledge for another house of our own. We found that there are many ways to save money building a house without sacrificing quality—we found out about them while and after we'd built, and we did make some dumb mistakes in the course of it. Looking at it positively, though, our lessons should help *you* save money and aggravation if you ever decide to try the retirement-village route yourself.

"I worked up a sheet on cost-saving ideas for some friends who built a house a couple years ago. They say it saved them thousands. Come to think of it, all I got from *them* was a bottle of wine, too. I think I work too cheap."

"Well, don't think about that now," I said. "Help your friend Richard before you start your consulting business."

"Okay," he said with seeming reluctance, "It's clear I'm not going to get anything out of *you*. How about if you remember me in your will?"

"Right," I said, "I'll be sure to do that, but I'm not sure what you're going to need money for at age 150."

"You never know," said Gordon. "Here's the scoop, anyway." He handed me the following:

CONSTRUCTION TIPS THAT WILL SAVE MONEY

1. When designing a house or buying plans, strive for 4-foot increments for exterior walls (e.g., 24 ft. by 40 ft. = 960 sq. ft.). Four-foot increments minimize the number of cuts, calculations, and overall waste during construction. To demonstrate how much this can save, consider a house that *doesn't* use the 4-foot increments and that requires cuts for walls, flooring, and roofing. Estimate 800 cuts to make the materials fit. Now, figure on four minutes per cut to take the measurements, position the material and cut it—that's 3,200 minutes, or 53 hours. At $30 per hour for a carpenter, you can save $1,590.

   The same idea works on the interior if you can save time on cutting materials for gyproc and other materials and finishes, etc.

2. Avoid too many corners and jogs in the residence—square or rectangular is much cheaper and you can still get an interesting look if you pick the right design. Here again, simplicity saves time. A crew of two journeymen carpenters and two helpers costs about $100 per hour. Complexity takes time, and those $100 hours quickly add up.

3. Select a simple roof line without dormers that meets the main roof structure at right angles. If you must have a change in roof pitch, try for a shedroof instead of peaked dormers that require complex angles and cuts. To create a covered porch, consider extending the roof line at the gable end and use posts and truss for support. Carpenters can easily spend two weeks on a complex roof while a straighter run can be done in half the time—remember those $100 hours.

4. Building a concrete slab, on grade, and not having a basement means that you sacrifice your home's square footage, but you save considerably on excavation costs. The slab on grade also facilitates gas-fired "infloor" hot-water heating, one of the best and most cost-efficient heating systems.

5. Give careful thought to finishings, plans, and storage needs. These can run up your construction bill very quickly too:

- For kitchen cabinets, shop around for quotes and quality.
- If you want hardwood in your living area or dining room, consider inlaying carpet in the center of the rooms and using the wood only around the perimeters as a "frame"— this saves hundreds or even thousands of dollars.
- Use stock plans if you can find ones you like. Architects cost big-time. You may have to have a local draftsperson adjust the plans to conform to regional building requirements, but the costs for these changes are usually nominal.
- If money is a concern, postpone some "dream features" until you have the money. You'll have more than enough to do finishing a home. The odd thing left unfinished for a few months or a year isn't the end of the world. For example, you can do hardwood or tile floors later and live with throw carpets on plywood for a while.
- For plumbing, keep kitchen and baths "back-to-back" to minimize the plumber's time and materials.
- Use outdoor space to expand the visuals of your living area. Decks and patios with windows help "bring the outside in." You could probably trim several hundred square feet of floor space easily if you spend time maximizing overall efficiency and creating storage spaces elsewhere. At a minimum of $60/sq. ft. and running as high as $100+/sq. ft., trimming 300 square feet would save you a lot of money.
- Plan for outdoor storage. Having all your storage inside is costly, again figuring a minimum of $60/sq. ft. This is especially true for storing items that can be kept somewhere cold as long as they're dry.

- Minimize strange window shapes—stock window sizes are cheaper .
- Take the time to investigate heating systems carefully. Natural gas is almost always cheaper than other heating fuels or electricity.
- One stage of construction where being extremely picky and demanding pays off is insulation and caulking. Careless work installing insulation around doors and windows and at the peaks of vaulted ceilings will lose you a lot of heat later on. Similarly, ensure that caulking around windows and doors, wherever heat can escape or cold can seep in, is done with the utmost precision. You'll save hundreds of dollars in only a few years with quality insulation and caulking work.
- Maximize glass on outside walls with southern exposure if possible to take advantage of passive solar light and heat. Again, this will cut heating costs when the sun is shining. Conversely, minimize glass on those parts of the house that face north.
- Do you need a separate laundry room? At $60/sq. ft. and assuming the average laundry room is about 30 sq.ft., that would cost you $1,800. Could you live with stacking machines in a 3-foot-by-3-foot closet-like space designed specifically for the purpose (save $1,260)?
- Minimize your use of interior walls. Modern interior design often provides for no walls between living areas, dining areas, and kitchens. Use walls only in rooms where you need privacy. For families concerned about both privacy and noise, open concepts are not always suitable. For retirees these concerns tend to be less important. Fewer walls mean less expense in interior finishing and make a house seem much larger than it really is.

Having finished reading about the cost-saving ideas, I thought it time to query Gordon about the macro view of village costs and other issues. He was happy to fill me in.

Finance

"Our development consists of a 10-acre parcel with 250 feet of waterfront. As I said before, we were approved for 20 dwellings, each lot being about one-third of an acre. The remainder of the land is common areas, and the access roads and driveways that run down each side. The cost of the property was $300,000. We spent another $100,000 for development costs, including the water system and sewage. At a total of $400,000, the cost worked out to be $20,000 per lot.

"By using stock plans, and watching construction costs as closely as we knew how, Sara and I managed to build the 960 sq. ft. house for $60/sq. ft. or $57,600. Village bylaws require an additional $7,000 from each owner to build the 3,000 sq. ft. common building and provide private storage rooms.

"Then, each owner placed $8,000 in a village trust account which we've invested in various interest-bearing instruments to generate the monthly revenue we need to support a part-time maintenance person for watering, cutting lawns, garbage collection, and snow removal. We review this maintenance pool of funds annually to make sure it's enough. Owners are expected to top it up if inflation pushes up costs. So far we've done better than 8 percent, so our return on the $160,000 is more than adequate. We're actually increasing the pot!

"Here's how all the costs broke down:

Lot	$20,000
House	$57,600
Storage	$ 2,000
Workshop/gym	$ 5,000
Maintenance deposit	$ 8,000
Total	**$92,600**

"If you ever build, you might also benefit from a detailed item-ization of the dozens of construction components you should price out carefully so you know what your costs are going to be before you commit. It's much more complete than any other I've seen. Those seemingly little things that many people leave out end up costing a lot of money, things like log treatments and the cost of cedar to trim out doors, windows, and baseboards. There's a few thousand dollars right there."

He handed me another sheet.

BUILDING COST BREAKDOWN

Lot cost (including legal fees)	$ _____
Felling trees/lot preparation	_____
Plans/state of title	_____
Construction insurance	_____
Building permit fee	_____
Appraisal for bank & mortgage fees	_____
Concrete slab and pad insulation	_____
Log work/erection/crane rental	_____
Carpentry	_____
Services: Sewer/Water	_____
Electrical	_____
Gas	_____
Insulation installation	_____
Siding	_____
Fireplace	_____
Windows/doors/knobs/locks	_____
Gyproc installation	_____
Concrete & form rental	_____
Labor basement/concrete work	_____
Excavation & fill	_____
Gutters/soffits/fascia	_____
Casual labor (siding, log treating, painting, etc.)	_____
Appliances	_____
Hot tub	_____
Bath mirrors, deck railings	_____
Temporary and permanent electrical services	_____
Cabinets: Kitchen/bath	_____
Building materials	_____
Plumbing/heating/fixtures	_____
Roofing (materials & labor)	_____
Flooring: Tile per sq. ft.	_____
Hardwood per sq. ft.	_____
Carpet per sq. yd.	_____
Landscaping, driveway	_____
Window coverings	_____
RUNNING TOTAL	$ _____
Minus Lot ($)	$ _____
GRAND TOTAL	$ _____
Cost per sq. foot =	$ _____ /sq. ft.

> The domestic Hearth. There only is real happiness.
> — Anatole France

Storage

"By stipulating that houses be single-story and not occupy more than 1,000 square feet of floor space, we do need storage space. So we built two rows of storage huts with 10 locked units of 200 square feet each. You probably saw the huts running down each side of the lot near the entrance and exit when you arrived. These give each owner access to a small dry, private space and are adequate if you're not too much of a packrat. They aren't heated or insulated and were quite inexpensive to build, about $2,000 for each resident."

Workshop

"One of the basic philosophies we entrenched in our village constitution was that residents should always have places to vent their creativity, or somewhere to do projects if they need to make more money in their retirement and can't do it in their cottages. So we built the community center that works as a social center, and a well-equipped metal and wood workshop and crafts center. It has sewing machines and a lot of other specialized equipment, too.

"Those who want to use the wood and metal shop and tools pay a fee of $10 a day. That permits them access to the rough workroom, used by us carpenters for cutting and assembly, and then there's a finishing room that's clean and dust-free for any projects that need to be stained, Varathaned, or painted.

"I usually make six or more coffee and end tables a month, and each takes me about five days in the shop. I simply build the $50 for the shop into my costs and it works out to be a lot cheaper than building a separate shop and outfitting it.

"This 2,000-square-foot building cost us $100,000, or $5,000 per resident. Without being luxurious, it's very functional."

Fitness Center

Gordon explained that residents at The Last Resort also decided in the early planning stages that they wanted a fitness center in their community center.

"We discussed it and came to the conclusion that we couldn't afford it at first, but within a year we changed our minds. Keeping ourselves physically fit is very important for obvious reasons," he said, "plus the 'sweat shop,' as we call it, serves an important social function.

"We added the 1,000 square feet onto the common building just recently. Each owner kicked in another $5,000 for it.

"It doesn't seem there would be enough people in the Resort to support all these amenities!" I had to say.

"Actually, you're right," he said, "and that's very astute of you to notice. There are only 20 cottages and 33 residents, half a dozen of whom have some health problems that don't permit them to use the equipment in the sweat shop. Actually, then, there are only a couple of dozen of us who use it, so the first question became, 'How can we get a fitness center that will support itself?'

"The answer was easy—sell 100 memberships to people from the surrounding area for $200 a year. That brings in $20,000 a year, enough to pay for the the center's equipment and decor finishings in the first year. Now we keep enough money aside to maintain the equipment and use the surplus to pay for the center's maintenance and upkeep. We've set up a cooperative arrangement so there's no profit and therefore no tax implications.

"The 100 memberships don't result in overcrowding at all—the gym is open from 6 a.m. to 10 p.m., so the external members and the residents add up to only 124 people or so. It seems that everyone rather enjoys having the people from outside come in. It helps de-emphasize what we otherwise might consider our isolation, which can be a concern and problem at some retirement villages.

"We also raise funds from renting the gathering room at the community center for small functions. We have a couple of people in the Resort who like to organize game nights and weekend flea markets. We collect donations from those events and make money off the things that are sold. The community center actually generates quite a nice bit of revenue and it gives us important outlets to keep busy organizing things and socializing."

Maintenance
"As I mentioned before, we have a part-time groundskeeper who looks after the common areas all year round. Each owner couple is responsible for their own lot. Each pays for any additional help we may need to look after our own environment beyond that."

Range of Services
"Retirement villages and developments can offer a very wide range of services, according to their residents' needs. At the moment no one needs serious nursing care but we have a committee looking at the types of things we may want to consider down the road. I have a list of services we've worked up so far."

He gave me another sheet.

POSSIBLE SERVICES

In home:

- chores (errands, yardwork)
- meals
- transportation
- companion
- outreach
- periodic home health care
- intermediate nursing for chronic health problems on an "as needed" basis

- housekeeping
- personal care (as needed)
- emergency response
- medications
- custodial nursing (full-time, onsite)
- skilled nursing
- hospice

Resident Age Limits

"To ensure that we maintain the controlled and quiet atmosphere we want, the minimum age limit of owners in the village is 55 years."

Selling

"Anyone who wants to sell a cottage is free to do so at market price, so long as the new resident meets the age requirement and is prepared to sign the agreement of understanding that details regulations and policies."

New Construction and Services

"Of course, residents are responsible for paying their share of all new construction, improvements, and services. We do try to keep these costs to an absolute minimum. To ensure fairness, we need to receive a 75-percent Yes vote from all owners before any new costs can be levied on residents. Interestingly, there were no dissenters for the community or fitness centers. Would-be owners must agree to honor this commitment before they take up residence here.

"As far as the health and personal care and assistance services we expect some of us may need over the coming decade, it appears likely that a 'user pay' system will be the most appropriate way of funding these. This may well change when a majority of residents eventually need assistance in whatever forms. Fortunately, we have some time to work something out in advance. At the same time this isn't something we want to ignore for much longer.

"So," he asked, "does that give you a feel for what we've done here and how we did it?"

"Yes," I answered. "As usual, it doesn't look like you guys have overlooked much."

"Planning," he said smiling. "It makes everything easier and the end result much better."

My mind was abuzz, as it had been from the moment I arrived.

Successful entrepreneurs in the future will be those who understand demographics and how to translate a good idea into wealth.

CHAPTER 10

Ace Up Your Sleeve: Entrepreneurship in Retirement

Chapter Goal: To make the case for entrepreneurship in retirement as a means of making money *and* having fun doing something you enjoy!

DAY 4, Morning

Another clear, sunny morning. I found Gordon sitting in his usual place on the deck with a thermos of hot coffee. I sat with a mug warming my hand and watched some villagers fly-fishing off the dock. Sporadic laughter echoed up from the beach. The trout were jumping.

Sara joined us and we sat quietly together sipping our coffee.

About a half hour later Gordon sighed and sat forward in his chair. "Okay. I think it's time we looked at your complete retirement portfolio to see how we can make you some more money and create some fun at the same time."

"Money and fun," I said. "The two don't seem to go together in my life."

"That's too bad," he said. "Mind you, they didn't for most of my life, either. It's only since we detired that we've really thought about how to make money by having fun."

"I'm all ears," I said.

"Yes, you might consider getting those fixed," he said, arching one eyebrow at me.

PLANNING ENTREPRENEURSHIP

"Okay, no sense of humor this morning, I see. Well, you've been out in our boat, and you know we take holidays every winter to sunny climes. What would you say if I told you half the expenses and capital costs we incur are tax-deductible?"

"I'd say, if this is legal tell me more."

"It's simple, really," he said. "The year we detired we formed a corporation that allows us to make some extra money and qualify for a host of deductions at the same time. For example, you've seen the rustic furniture made of driftwood and other outdoor collectibles spread all over the house. Well, we use the boat every spring, summer, and fall to beachcomb in search of all that stuff. Then, on rainy days or whenever the urge strikes me, I turn it into furniture and pieces of artwork, which I then sell in a dozen stores here in the West Kootenay, Vancouver, Banff, and a couple others in the States.

"Because I'm making several thousand dollars a year from these wooden creations, and since the boat is used at least half-time to collect the raw materials, one-half of the cost of the boat is tax-deductible, plus half all the other expenses it takes to run it. That takes a lot of the financial pain out of owning a boat, and the beachcombing gives us a good reason for getting out into the fresh air.

"Frankly, just motoring around or cruising up to beaches to sit and read a book all day would get quite boring. We both really enjoy the search for unusual pieces and get a lot of satisfaction out of making them into things that are useful or just nice to look at. The other very real bonus is the several thousand dollars a year that comes in from the sales."

"Interesting," I said, "but I'm not very handy with tools. I'd probably end up with several fewer digits if you let me loose with a powersaw. I'm more interested, though, in how you write off any costs by heading down south to the sun."

"Equally easy," he said. "The furniture and artwork are part of it, since we do sell to people we've met in California and Arizona—so part of each trip is marketing and research. Sara has started a small import/export operation too, also through our corporation, so every time we travel we make sure it's to some-place where we can look for merchandise to import and also for manufacturers in the U.S. and Mexico interested in shipping to us in Canada. We then offer these goods at wholesale prices to another dozen retail stores we've cultivated relations with."

"Boy," I said, "it doesn't sound like you've retired at all! Doesn't all that keep you kind of busy?"

"Not really," said Gordon. "We love to tour around the lake. Making the furniture and artwork is something I would do even if I didn't get paid for it. And the travel is much more interesting now that we have useful things to do when we get there. Neither of us could golf every day or just sit around, so we get to meet all kinds of stimulating business people, make some money while we're doing it, and write off a good chunk of the costs.

"Most people don't realize it," he continued, "but knowing how to set up a simple business and take advantage of corporate tax deductions can make you, and save you, thousands of dollars a year and let you have fun while you're at it."

Deducing Your Deductions

I began to see some possibilities for my writing.

"I guess I could claim some deductions for the writing I do. I've had only a couple of major clients for the past five years—I guess I haven't taken advantage of all the tax breaks I could have realized."

"What have you claimed?" asked Gordon.

"Well, my computer and vehicle mileage and any telephone calls or other directly related expenses. It's all kind of complicated because I get reimbursed by the clients and have been told I can't get reimbursed and claim deductions at the same time."

"You do have to be careful you never run afoul of the taxman," said Gordon, "but as long as you can pass Revenue Canada's definition of a self-employed person, you qualify for a whole lot of deductions that can save you a lot of money. I'll show you.

"This is a guide I put together for my own reference. Of course these percentages can change, so you do have to keep up with them year to year.

Tax Deductibles

1. Motor vehicle: Capital depreciation, insurance, gas, and maintenance, all to whatever percentage the vehicle is used for business purposes (say 50-percent business use equals 50-percent write-offs for all the items listed). You must keep accurate mileage records of all your business trips and travel.

2. Home office: All equipment, furniture, and office supplies, either as depreciated items or complete write-offs, such as supplies. This includes "asset conversion," which means you can claim "fair market value/cost" on items and equipment you had before you started the business. This can include furniture, equipment, and all office supplies right down to scissors, pencils, paper, tape. There is usually at least $1,000 worth of supplies in any home office. The key to keeping the tax people happy is to establish values that are fair and reasonable.

Don't forget books you buy as part of your professional-development library. You can't claim full price on old books, but you can reasonably claim one-half of their value. One hundred books can mean another $1,000 in write-offs.

3. Mortgage interests: The percentage of your house you use exclusively for your home office can be deducted from your taxable income (so if your home office occupies 10 percent of your home's total square footage, you can deduct 10 percent of your mortgage interest as a business expense).

4. Other expenses:

- Accounting
- Bad debts
- Fuel
- Interest and bank charges
- Licenses and permits
- Maintenance & repairs
- Depreciation & replacements
- Stamps/stationery
- Trade association dues
- Travel (meals, accommodation, etc.)

- Advertising
- Freight/cartage
- Insurance (auto/house)
- Legal & audit
- Light & power
- Operating supplies
- Rent
- Subscriptions
- Telephone, fax
- Tools used

"Sheesh, there's a lot to claim!" I said, surprised.

"Absolutely," said Gordon. "This little list is worth a lot of money. And it's not even complete, since every business will have different deductions it can reasonably claim.

"As far as taking advantage of the tax write-offs, I should make one very important point. Revenue Canada gets really cranky with people who start businesses just for the tax advantages. There is one rule of thumb to remember—the business should have genuine potential to make money and you should be prepared to commit sufficient time and planning to ensure it does. Successive losses will be sure to get you audited and could cost you a lot of money. That isn't the goal."

Love That Leverage

"Something else that is very important to understand in entrepreneurship is the power of leverage."

"How so?" I asked.

"Well, many people have a strange attitude about borrowing money, especially once they're retired. Sometimes it makes perfect sense to borrow, though.

"For example, many people will take money out of their savings, or, as many retirees do, out of their RRIFs, to pay cash for things associated with starting a business. Conversely, they'll then turn right around and borrow money to buy a car or fix their houses."

"Is that bad?"

"Not if you like throwing money away," he said. "Let me continue.

"Suppose someone wants to launch a business that will cost $10,000 to start. The aspiring entrepreneur takes the money out of her RRIF. Now she has the cash to start the business, but she has $10,000 *less* in her RRIF principal and she has no corresponding expenses to write off yet.

"That $10,000 would have earned $600, tax-sheltered, in the first year at 6-percent interest. Compounding the $10,000 over 5 years would have grown her $13,382, or a gain of $3,382. That money is now gone. And, everything her business earns, over and above its expenses, becomes taxable income.

"Consider this scenario instead:

"She borrows the $10,000. Let's assume a five-year payback period at 9-percent interest with monthly payments of $206.79. The total interest charges over the term of the loan would be $2,407.40, which averages out to $481.48 a year.

"All of the interest on the loan is tax-deductible, so a person in the 40-percent tax bracket would pay $192.59 less in taxes through having the loan—that's $963 over five years. Add the tax rebate to the sheltered RRIF growth, and the credit side of the ledger totals $4,344 over the five-year period. That's a significant gain if you simply deduct the cost of the loan interest of $2,407.40. Net gain—$1,936.60.

"I'd say a person has to be crazy or simply lack my trusty calculator to take money out of a tax-sheltered investment instead of taking out a loan in such an instance. You gotta love that leverage."

I wasn't quite following yet, but I was intrigued.

"I assume you borrowed money for your furniture business?" I asked.

"You bet," said Gordon. "Same line of reasoning. After we figured out our business plan it was pretty clear we could gross about $12,000 a year in furniture sales, about half of which would be net. We estimated we'd have to spend $5,000 on tools and would claim one-half the cost of the boat, or another $12,500. So, we borrowed $17,500 over five years at 9-percent interest with monthly payments of $361.88. The interest on the loan amounts to about $843 a year, which we use to reduce our taxable income. That saves us $337 a year.

"As in the previous scenario, we accumulate $5,919 interest in our RRIF over the same five-year period plus the $337 tax rebate each year from writing off the interest. So, the credits come to $7,604 over five years while the interest is only $4,212.80. We're $3,391.20 better off."

"Wow!" I blurted. "I've never really understood how borrowing money could actually make money, but I must admit your argument makes sense. Obviously, I've got to think about how this can work for me."

"You definitely should," he said. "Most people roll their eyes when you suggest that they start a retirement business. Yet after a bit of discussion, as you identify their personal interests and skills, the ones they enjoy, and you follow that up with some explanation about tax advantages, you often have a new, interested entrepreneur.

"I have to add at this point that while running a small business isn't for everyone, a lot of people who are suited don't get into it simply because they don't understand what's involved and how it could benefit them. Once you've had a business that makes you extra money, and saves you even more at tax time, you'll wonder why you didn't run a business out of your home a lot sooner."

"I imagine the hardest thing for a lot of people is thinking up what kind of business they would *like* to run in retirement," I suggested.

"You're right," said Gordon, "but there are dozens of little businesses that can be fun for retirees and have small startup costs. Here's a variety of so-called hot businesses for the nineties that almost anyone could run depending on education and general experience."

BUSINESS IDEAS

- Retirement counseling
- Products for the aging
- Retiree services
- Inputting/word processing
- Managing vending machines
- Clothing alterations
- Maintaining plants
- Painting signs
- Customizing closets
- Selling at flea markets
- Producing astrological scrolls
- Creating party lawn signs
- Art: any kind
- Hobby: anything that may sell
- Pet care
- Gardening: selling fresh produce, flowers
- Book publishing
- Carpentry
- Consulting: wide range
- Crafts
- Selling & installing alarms
- Planning seniors' recreation
- Tutoring
- Framing pictures
- Putting together gift baskets
- Installing safety surfaces on sidewalks, tubs, showers, etc.
- Advertising specialties
- Arranging and conducting guided tours
- Desktop publishing
- Home sitting
- Daycare: (suitable for younger retirees)

"Obviously, you're limited only by your imagination. The point is that anyone looking for a business to start in retirement should think carefully about that statistic of 100 million North Americans being over the age of 55 by 2011. That's a huge market! And it will mean a lot of new needs and immense disposable income. If you can come up with a marketable product or service, you'll be able to make that extra cash to take those holidays in Hawaii.

"And, speaking of demand, that's another of my incontrovertible rules that I like to bore people with. A business that hopes to make money has to be BIIQ."

"BIIQ—right," I said. "Cosmo told me about your BIIQ, but it escapes me now exactly what it stands for."

"BIIQ," he said, "stands for Benefits, Interest, and Impact Quotient. Simply put, it means that if you want to sell people something, they had better be able to see immediately how it will benefit them, interest them, or have some impact on their lives. If it ain't BIIQ, it ain't saleable. I'm always amazed at how many businesses don't seem to understand this essential concept.

"As you know, everything we do requires making plans first. Our furniture business was no different. We wanted to assure ourselves it had a chance of making money before we invested in the boat, tools, and other materials. So, we did our market research and put together a business plan. If you think you might ever look at starting a new business, or at doing research or putting together a formal plan I have sample sheets you can have."

"Why not?" I said, "As long as things are still free."

"Your credit is rapidly running out.

"You'll notice that the top sheets deal with market research. It made sense to us that we do that first to find out if our idea had any chance of success. If an idea doesn't hold up in the research stage, you have to rework it to boost consumer demand for your products or services or scrap the idea completely.

"Our business plan may be more detailed than you would need yourself, but it's better to have too much information rather than too little. This one grew out of several sessions I had with a friend who wanted to start a business. He needed to come up with a format to qualify him for financing. You may not need financing, but having the entire plan can't hurt. Just use the parts that are relevant to you, particularly those about researching the marketplace and preparing your marketing plan."

He handed me another sheaf of papers.

SIMPLE "ONE PERSON" MARKET RESEARCH

Many business people base their business decisions on "instinct" rather than hard facts. The results are often unsatisfactory; these people lose money, and their businesses fail. By yielding critical information before start-up, market research can save you a lot of grief. Information you need:

1. Who are your target audiences?
2. Is your product or service in demand?
3. How will prospective customers want it delivered?
4. What price will they pay?
5. How often are they likely to patronize your business?
6. How will you differentiate your business from others' to improve your chances of success?
7. Where will you get materials, supplies, products, etc.?

THE STEPS IN MARKET RESEARCH

1. Identify clearly your product line and/or service.
2. Gather secondary data from Stats Canada, manufacturers, suppliers, wholesalers, association or government reports/studies that focused on similar businesses. Visit your local library and call

---

Stats Canada 1-800 numbers. Included in secondary data are studies of demographics (age, sex, population, income, population growth) and psychographics (the study of lifestyles, attitudes, expectations, "trending," what's hot).

3. If the secondary data is encouraging, establish a schedule and a budget for collecting your primary data.
4. Design and test a primary-research questionnaire.
5. Gather primary data.
6. Tabulate and analyze the data.
7. Develop your business action plan after you have some defensible proof that your idea can succeed.

A Harvard Business School Study into business failures revealed that:

1. 32% failed because of inadequate research and development.
2. 23% failed because they were bad ideas.
3. 14% failed owing to uncontrolled costs.
4. 13% failed because of weak marketing strategies.
5. 10% failed because of bad timing
6. 8% failed owing to increased activity from competitors.

SAMPLE "RESEARCH APPROACH"

1. Show samples of your product line or carefully describe your service to as many people as possible from the target groups that are most likely to buy, and from the geographic areas in which you will operate. Ensure you cover all target groups— age, sex, income levels—as broadly as possible. The survey respondents should be objective "strangers." Choose about 100 people to survey—don't scrimp on the number of respondents

or the validity of your information will suffer. This can lead you astray in your projections.

2. Ask questions such as the following, always in the same order and in the same way, to improve your data's reliability.

   a) "Given what you now know about the product/service, we want to determine your potential as a customer. If the product/service were available, how likely would you be to buy it?

      1) Would certainly buy
      2) Quite certain I would buy
      3) Might buy
      4) Slight possibility I would buy
      5) Not likely I would buy
      6) Definitely would not buy"

   b) If a person responds to questions 4 to 6, ask: "What do you think would have to be changed to interest you in wanting or needing the product/service?"

   c) Do you currently buy or use a similar product or service? If a respondent answers Yes, ask: "Are you satisfied with it/your supplier? Have you experienced any problems? How could your product or service supplier serve you better?"

   d) "Our plans call for a price on our product/service of $[price]. How does this compare with what you now pay, or, if you don't use a similar product or service, how much do you think you would pay for such a product/service?"

   e) "How often do you think you would be likely to buy the product or service? In a week? In a month? In a year?"

   f) "Where or how would you be most likely to buy the product or service: at a retail store, at a fair, by mail order, etc.?"

Now you have the information you want to know how many people are likely to buy your product/service.

3. From question a) count the number of "Would certainly buy" and "Quite certain I would buy" responses. Not everyone who answered "Certainly" *will* buy, but it is reasonable to assume that about one-half of these people, and about 10 percent of those who answered "Quite certain," would actually buy if given the opportunity, place, price, and time.

Let's assume you have interviewed 100 people and received the following responses to question a):

If 20 people responded "Would certainly buy," you have 10 high-quality potential buyers. If 10 answered "Quite certain I would buy," assume one additional buyer. Assume only 5 percent of the "Might buy" responses would result in a sale. There were 15 of these responses, or .75 percent.

The calculations produce a total of about 11.75 likely buyers—11.75 percent of your sample *might* buy your product or service *if you got it to market so they had easy access to it and at a price they find agreeable.* (Note: This research design comes with no guarantees, but it is vastly superior to no prospective buyer research at all.)

The question now is, "How many buyers will it take to make a profitable business?" To answer this question you need precise knowledge of costs and profit margins. Then, by observing buyer traffic or by estimating population numbers in your target audiences, you have to figure out how long it would take to get the number of sales you need to pay all your expenses and make a profit. For example, in a given month, do you need 200 buyers to spend $100 each, or 2,000 buyers to spend $2 each? Does your research tell you this?

You must also try to estimate how much of the "market share" you are likely to gain. For example, if there are three businesses like yours you might expect, within a reasonable period of time, and if you choose the right location and market your product or service competently, to acquire 33⅓ percent of buyers for a particular product or service. Knowing what percentage of people are likely to buy and estimating your market share gives you some idea of your potential revenue.

Obviously, if your research indicates that potential Yes customers would not produce sufficient income for your needs, do not proceed any further unless you can reposition, re-target, and generally rethink your proposed product and/or service.

4. If the decision is a go, you want to know at what price it will succeed in the marketplace. From your sample of 100 people determine the price range your potential customers expect. Then ask yourself, "Can I provide the product(s) or services for this price and make a profit?"
5. Once you have settled on your price range, you have to accurately calculate your costs of goods (COGs) or cost per service unit—the total costs of space, materials, equipment, utilities, transportation, wages, insurance, advertising, interest charges, office supplies, taxes, and so on. Can you sell at the price the marketplace demands, and can you earn enough profit to make the venture worth your while?

A guide for start-up businesses: Aim for revenue to exceed your costs by a factor of at least two. You should insist that your research support this ratio. You *do not* want to find yourself with overhead and the cost of replacing goods sold equal to or more than your revenues! In the planning stage, when many people tend to be too optimistic, always overestimate your costs and underestimate your revenue. For example, if your costs per month of operation are $1,000, including cost of goods or delivering services, your research should suggest a projected revenue of at least $2,000. You should build in that cushion of comfort or you could find yourself in immediate trouble. Start-up is usually slower than expected.

COMPREHENSIVE BUSINESS AND FINANCIAL PLAN

Business Plan Format

1. Covering letter should include:
   a) company name, address, telephone number(s)
   b) main point of your presentation
   c) company description: nature of business, market area
   d) financial overview: collateral, names and addresses of investors, inventory, available capital, real estate, equity
   e) business loan being sought: amount sought, term, line of credit, mortgage, leasing
   f) summary of how you propose to use the funds
   g) name of contact person and telephone number

2. Attached summary page—Highlights of Business Plan:
   a) project/company objectives
   b) products and services
   c) competitive advantages (SWOT Analysis (Strengths, Weaknesses, Opportunities, and Threats), Environmental Scan)
   d) market potential
   e) assessment of competition (SWOT Analysis and Environmental Scan)
   f) management/business experience and talents (SWOT Analysis)
   g) "bottom line" needs
   h) percentage/return on investment and when

3. Market Analysis:
   a) industry and geographic area outlook and growth potential
   b) new developments: demographics and economic trends
   c) sources of research information
   d) size of total market
   e) sales revenue projected
   f) anticipated market share
   g) new requirements of the marketplace
   h) market trends: in 1 year, in 5 years, in 10 years
   i) technological trends
   j) changing needs of society/clients
   k) buying patterns: why to buy, when to buy, expectations, income
   l) weaknesses and strengths of the competition
   m) risk evaluation

4. Description of Your Business Venture:
   a) how product/service has been developed to fill niche identified
   b) special characteristics (differentiation)
   c) methods of operation (operations plans)
   d) local and regional potential
   e) competitive advantage: niche, uniqueness
   f) business location and size
   g) size of premises, property
   h) sole proprietorship, partnership, limited/incorporated company
   i) patents, trademarks, copyrights
   j) home or office
   k) staff: how many, full- or part-time
   l) personal experience, talents (via résumé)
   m) wholesale, retail, service
   n) suppliers
   o) service policies: credit/collection, guarantees

    p) costing, mark-ups, margins, break-even
    q) commission staff, agents, sub-consultants
    r) quality control procedures
    s) cash-flow analysis
    t) seasonal variations

5. Marketing and Sales Strategies:
    a) overview of marketing plan
    b) marketing vehicles and strategies
    c) sales tools/support/approach
    d) advertising and promotion options
    d) tracking and evaluation

6. Business Goals:
    a) strategic plan

7. Supporting Professional Assistance:
    a) lawyer
    b) accountant
    c) banker
    d) insurance agent
    e) marketing specialist

8. Appendices
    a) name of current banking institution and types of accounts
    b) personal statement of net worth
    c) business and personal insurance coverage
    d) legal agreements
    e) copies of promotional materials
    f) testimonial letters of support
    g) credit status information

Finance Plan and Funding Requests

1. Summary
   a) of the whole proposal
   b) of yourself, your experience, and skills
   c) of your business concept
   d) of your financing needs
   e) of how you will use and repay the funds

2. Financial Condition Synopsis:
   a) owner's equity
   b) cash position
   c) outstanding financial commitments
   d) breakdown of current expenses by category
   e) your grasp of financial concepts

3. Financial Plan for the Future:
   a) projected balance sheets for the next 3 years
   b) projected income statements
   c) cash-flow projections

4. Reasons Why You Need Financing:
   a) what period the financial plan covers
   b) what precisely the money will achieve

Business Plan Checklist

1. Introductory letter

2. Title page

3. Executive summary

4. Background information: legal status of firm, start-up

5. Description of the industry:
   - principal characteristics
   - trends
   - players
   - barriers

6. Description of product or service:
   - assessment of strengths and weaknesses (SWOT Analysis)
   - patents, trademarks, copyright protection
   - technology you will be using

7. Description of management team:
   - organizational chart
   - curricula vitae
   - management compensation

8. Your marketing plan:
   - assessment of total market
   - assessment of target market
   - assessment of competition
   - assess marketing advantage
   - pricing policy
   - selling policy
   - distribution policy
   - advertising/promotion plan
   - services and warranties

9. Description of land, buildings, equipment:
   - location
   - value
   - requirements

10. Description of how you will operate:
    - work flow
    - inventory control
    - supplies and materials

11. Personal references

12. A financial plan:
    - capital requirements
    - sources of financing
    - cash-flow projections
    - projected income statements
    - break-even chart

13. Risks and problems faced by business and plans for coping:
    - worst-case scenarios
    - risk avoidance strategies
    - impact of risk

"Well," I said, "as with everything else we've covered these past few days, you favor a pretty formal planning process. Do you think this amount of detail is really necessary, though? I wouldn't think that many retirees would need, or want, to borrow money for their business ideas. And if this is the case, why prepare an elaborate business plan that no one but they will read?"

"I understand your point," said Gordon. "Nonetheless I still think it's a wise process to follow. Even if you intend to start only a small one-person business and have no debt or others involved, the discipline of preparing a comprehensive plan ensures that you've examined all the angles carefully. As I mentioned earlier, the purpose of the entrepreneurial exercise in retirement is to earn extra money to supplement your income. This money should let you enjoy some extras that you might not be able to afford otherwise.

"A key point, though, is that running a business enables you to take write-offs to reduce the amount of income tax you pay. This is where having the detailed plan really pays off. It *forces* you to look carefully at whether or not the business has a reasonable chance of being profitable. Think of it as the litmus test the government applies when deciding whether or not to allow the tax deductions you claim by it.

"In other words a good plan helps launch a good business. It makes no sense for you to cut corners just to reduce your taxes. If there's any discernible pattern in a succession of unsuccessful businesses, it's that Revenue Canada quickly becomes suspicious of a person's real intentions in setting up a business. The object of the exercise is not to spark a tax audit and end up having several years' worth of deductions disallowed. Who needs the hassle? Whether your proposed business is big or small, plan your work and then work your plan."

CHAPTER 11

Wrapping It All Up

DAY 4, Afternoon

My flight was leaving in a few hours. I'd be home for supper. I was as eager to see Lorraine as I was saddened to be leaving friends who had given so much to me so selflessly during my visit. I was sorry, too, to be leaving The Last Resort. Life there felt calm and comforting. The highways, traffic, concrete, hordes of people, and air pollution to which I would be returning didn't appeal at all. What a difference a few days can make.

As I stood at the patio railing thinking these thoughts Gordon and Cosmo came up behind me. Gordon laid his arm across my shoulders.

"We're going to miss you. It's been really nice getting reacquainted. I know we didn't get as much time to kibbitz around as I originally thought, but you seemed willing to make this a working vacation. I only hope you got enough out of it to make it worth your while."

"Enough out of it? You guys have no idea how important these four days have been to me. My brain is full to the point of aching! I feel as if I've got a whole new lease on life—I mean life now *and* life at retirement. I thought Lorraine and I were planning pretty well, even if our figures were a bit skewed. Wow. Our version of planning seems pretty pathetic now. I arrived feeling so pessimistic about our future. Now I have a whole new outlook on things. I'm sorry to say goodbye to you, Sara, and Cosmo, but the information I've got in my head and grubby little hands will be invaluable."

"Well, Gord," said Cosmo, "it sounds like goose-hopper got his money's worth."

"Yeah, well, at the price we charged him he didn't have to get much. I always said people get what they pay for."

"In this case I've got to say your words of wisdom don't apply! Now that I know what is at stake I would have been willing to pay a lot for this crash course."

"Interesting," said Cosmo. "How would you summarize what you got out of all this? What do you think you'll do differently now?"

I gawked at him.

"What do you want, a list?"

"Sure, I'm curious to know exactly what made sense and seems most worthwhile to you. We talked for hours and hours. It's always tough to know what's really sinking in or what people think is important. Consider your wrap-up as payment for our efforts."

"Okay," I said, considering. "You asked for it. It just so happens I've kept a little diary of this visit. In it I've jotted down the highlights that I want to make sure I remember to pass on to Lorraine. I'll get it."

I grabbed my notebook from the bedroom and returned to the patio. Gordon and Cosmo were sitting at the table and Sara sat in a hanging chair. She was gently swinging herself back and forth with a big toe hooked into the back of Gordon's chair.

"The floor is all yours, goose-hopper," said Cosmo.

"All right, I'll approach what I've learned chronologically. That's the way I wrote up my notes."

<u>27 LESSONS TO TAKE HOME</u>

Lesson #1: Detirement Banish the word "retirement" from my vocabulary. Reversing the emphasis, even if just through a new prefix, places a different mental mindset on a stage of life that can and should be enjoyable and offer us the same kinds of fun and freedom that we knew at the beginning of our lives and through our teen years.

Lesson #2: Living space After seeing what Gord and Sara have done with 960 square feet, I wonder what in the hay we're doing in a house two and a half times that size. I think it's a safe bet it will be going on the market before the year 2000 and that anything new we build will be just as luxurious but a lot more efficient in terms of both functional space and cost.

Lesson #3: A new winery Having consumed a reasonable amount of wine these past four days I've got to say I see no reason to patronize the liquor store in future. We have lots of space in the basement, complete with sink and shelves. I did a quicky calculation the other night that eight bottles of wine a month at a cost of $8 instead of $64 will save us something in the neighborhood of $50,000 over 40 years. The simple arithmetic savings would be $26,880, but I'm estimating that we'll put that money to better use and that it will at least double. I never thought I could save money without cutting down on consumption.

Lesson #4: Strip-bond planning I don't know what Lorraine's going to think of switching a fair chunk of our RRSPs out of equities and into strip bonds, but the argument is pretty compelling. They also make long-term planning so simple that they're worth a closer look. What will make our decision much easier, of course, is interest rates spiking up in the next couple of years as equities become less viable.

Lesson #5: Investment time frame? Our entire lives One of the most important lessons I learned was to look at our investment horizon as 40 years, not 20 years. The extra 20 years makes all the difference between getting there and never getting there, not to mention all the difference to our peace of mind today.

Lesson #6: Demographics Up to now, I'd always viewed these as an arcane statistical morass. Now I see how important it is to think about what effects the bulge of aging boomers will have on us. I don't want to get caught on the wrong side of any of the housing or investment shifts those 100 million people over age 55 are going to cause.

Lesson #7: Retired but disabled It makes very little sense to wait until we're disabled before we spend a good portion of our detirement funds on travel and other pursuits that depend on good physical health. I suspect we aren't going to wait to enjoy our most active detirement years.

Lesson #8: Where we're going to live We'd always assumed that we'd live in the Lower Mainland. Now, just the thought of going back to the smog leaves me cold. I'll swap that for this any day of the week, thank you very much.

Lesson #9: Our city house assets Along with the aesthetic advantages of getting out of the big city I now recognize the very real financial considerations, too. I knew our house represented our largest single asset, but I never really thought about how we could use that to our detirement advantage. From now on, I'm going to consider that house a big fat $150,000 bill.

Lesson #10: Saving by the inch Looking at the planning process one year at a time has been an incredible mental shift. Before there were just all these far-off years and that huge, seemingly impossible amount of money that we had to sock away. Picking off the challenge year by year makes the process much more manageable. With luck and planning, we can get the after-65 funds in place and then start knocking off each year before we turn 65 to see if we can retire earlier.

Lesson #11: Looking at all the retirement income I had always looked at only our RRSPs as our detirement assets. Sara and Gordon have shown me that there are other sources—additional RRSP contributions for 20 years, our house, and the CPP if we can make sure successive governments don't ever think of fiddling with what we have all assumed is an unimpeachable moral contract.

Lesson #12: Worksheets for future expenditures/income Some books on the market discuss doing these calculations, although I'd never completed one. Doing so should be priority number one for those who really want to get an accurate picture of what they'll need and what'll likely be there when they need it.

Lesson #13: Using RRSP overcontribution allowances It was quite a shock to see how using our $2,000 each today could translate into a $40,000 strip bond 32 years down the road. It seems stupid not to take advantage of that tax shelter while we have the chance.

Lesson #14: "The Forgo Three Raises Plan" We're trying to put away $10,000 each year between the two of us and in the first few years, until we got used to the discipline, it was quite a stretch. I like the idea of automatically diverting three raises and the tax rebates automatically into an RRSP account. If people redirect this money *before* they get into the habit of spending it, and work it into their monthly budgets, most could get along quite well without those three raises—particularly when they consider the benefits they'll get at the other end, at retirement.

Lesson #15: Non-RRSP savings I don't know how much money we'll be able to save outside our RRSPs. With 20 years to go, I suspect just budgeting for it is all we need to do. Securing an extra $10,000 to $20,000 a year in detirement income might ensure we can afford those 12-star hotels on the Mediterranean. And, given that I am self-employed and don't always produce sufficient taxable income to qualify for the RRSP maximum contributions, putting money away outside the RRSPs may be the only way I can ensure I don't take the easy way out.

As a matter of fact, I think I know where there's about $20,000 lurking right now. A friend has a nice old BMW I can pick up for chump change. I wouldn't be surprised if Lorraine couldn't downscale to something cheaper, too, that would still provide us with good, reliable transportation. If that 20 grand invested now let us retire a year earlier, I wouldn't miss my Volvo one bit!

Lesson #16: Strategic Life & Investment Planning We'll always owe Cosmo a huge debt for introducing me to these concepts. Mushy planning produces mushy results. I've been way too mushy about this stuff all my life. Now I'm going to get SLIPing. Sara and Gordon and Cosmo have successfully made the case that money isn't everything. Without memorable experiences and daily joy, life is pointless.

Lesson #17: Stocks outside RRSPs, safer instruments in I'd heard about this before, too. Now I really appreciate the fact that a loss in your RRSP is permanent and not tax-deductible as an investment loss. Add to this that you can deduct interest from taxable income for buying stocks outside an RRSP and I'm converted.

Lesson #18: Absorb brokerage fees outside an RRSP I also know how important it is to keep every tax-sheltered dollar I can in my RRSP. So, knowing that I can buy stocks outside and pay the brokerage fees outside, and then transfer the entire allowable RRSP contribution inside an RRSP is a strategy worth quite a few thousand dollars over several decades.

Lesson #19: How to help my friends and relatives The worksheets and insights Sara and Gordon gave me help tremendously. I think I've absorbed enough to be able to get some other people who are close to me on a better track themselves. Consider me a disciple out there spreading the good word. I'll be surprised if Gary, my fisherman friend, and my niece don't feel a lot better after they see where they could stand. However, I think I'll extract more than a cheap bottle of wine from them for my efforts. . . .

Lesson #20: Stock Approaches For an Edge (SAFE) I'm sorry to say that our stock selections in the past have been based on what looked hot at the time or what investment counselors told us. Given the SAFE concept and knowing what to look for ourselves, and, more important, what questions to ask, makes me feel a lot more confident about choosing stocks. I want those stocks that show facts and fundamentals working in their favor. I'm going to put my "gut" out to pasture.

Lesson #21: Last Resort II I've got to bring Lorraine here. I want to show her what Gordon, Sara, Cosmo and others have done. I know she'll love it on first visit. I intend to start scouting out friends and acquaintances who may like the idea. I'll call Russ Waters, your realtor friend, first to ask him to keep an eye out for parcels of land suitable for a similar development. It's a long-term project and a little early to buy, but I don't want to wait too long to get moving on it. I agree about the likelihood of the exodus of people from big cities shortly after the year 2000. Alternatively, maybe Sara and Gordon and Cosmo won't mind us as neighbors if one of the units here comes up for sale about 10 years from now.

Lesson #22: Building tips While I've never built a new house, the tips Gordon lays out step by step can obviously save a lot of money when I finally do turn some sod. I can work around simpler roof lines and such to chop $10,000 off the cost of a cottage. Seeing what Sara and Gordon and Cosmo have done is inspiring. Somebody should start drying logs for our new residence today.

Lesson #23: Detirement entrepreneurship Like Sara and Gordon, I have skills that are marketable as long as my brain works. I should be able to parlay those talents into some cash. If I can make money, have fun, and take advantage of the write-offs on trips and such, I can't imagine not doing it.

Lesson #24: Love that leverage I think I've also, finally, gained an understanding of how borrowing money can be more profitable than using cash, especially if the cash is in a tax-sheltered environment. My first job when I get home will be to go downtown and buy one of those fancy calculators and a spreadsheet program for my computer. I'll be a competent number cruncher by the next time we meet.

I looked up at my audience. "And I have a few other observations of my own."

Lesson #25: Long-term rates may not get any better Current thinking calls for going short-term on bonds on the assumption that inflation may return and drive rates higher than they are now. However, with baby boomers becoming more conservative with their retirement investments, there could well be a big influx of money going into bonds, starting about 2005. Such a surplus of savings may actually drive rates *down*. If that happens, the roughly 8.5-percent yields on strip bonds today could end up being quite attractive and worth locking into.

Lesson #26: Holiday homeswaps to save hotel costs In working up our expense projections at retirement Lorraine and I would, under our original plan, spend thousands of dollars each year renting hotel rooms. I remember friends of ours who got their hands on a publication of worldwide listings of people interested in swapping their houses for a few months each year. For example, our friends swapped a cottage in the Okanagan for a villa on the Spanish Riviera in a two-month "win-win" for both parties, eliminating the prohibitive cost of hotels.

I think this kind of arrangement will be more common in future. I want to keep in mind having something nice here in Canada that would be in demand to people from countries where we'd like to holiday ourselves. The major snag, as I see it, is that we want to get away from January to April, so we'd have to find people from sunny climes who would want to come to Canada to visit friends or family, or ski or enjoy some other cold-weather sport, since we don't do a lot of beach-sitting during those months. Still, it may be practical.

Lesson 27: You owe yourself a debt I saved this one for last because I believe it's the most important of the whole lot. If young people were taught by their parents, school teachers, and employers that they have a priority debt as soon as they start working, to *themselves*, we wouldn't have so many fifty-year-olds trying to play retirement catch-up. Really, if people started life accepting that the top 10 percent of every paycheck automatically disappeared into the great retirement void, they could forget about needing any government programs. They could also start planning their luxury trips and pastimes about age 55. If anyone ever invents a time machine, I'm going back and doing it right.

I had finally finished. Satisfied, I looked up expectantly. Gordon, Sara, and Cosmo were all smiling and nodding their heads.

Sara spoke first. "It looks like we did a pretty decent job."

"And I thought he was sleeping," said Cosmo.

"I think he'll be the new detirement investment counselor at The Last Resort," added Gordon.

"I think it's also time for a final toast," said Sara, jumping up and disappearing into the cottage. She emerged with a bottle of champagne and four frosted glasses shaped like tulips.

Pop. Glasses filled and foaming.

"This is my toast," I said.

They all looked at me, waiting.

"In remembrance of a very productive four days and in honor of three wonderful people who have helped reshape two lives, and many others, that needed reshaping. I'll never forget your wisdom or your warm hospitality."

The drive back to the airport and the flight home are now bittersweet memories. Bitter because one never likes to separate from a place where every day is replete with joy, and sweet because I have a new sense of confidence in our abilities to take control of our lives and our futures.

Our days, weeks and months now are full of many more regular good memories. I had listened well.

If expectation is half the joy, we can take great comfort in knowing that the best plan we can make will be in the form of our own Last Resort.

With years a richer life begins,
The spirit mellows:
Ripe age gives tone to violins,
Wine, and good fellows.

— John Townsend Trowbridge

Afterword

Most authors aspire to send their readers worthwhile messages. At the same time, I can honestly say that the process of assembling the information for *The Last Resort* has been a very valuable learning experience for me. It forced me to crystallize my own vague concepts and build a framework within which to apply them.

The real reward, however, would be to find that the thoughts contained between these covers helped even one other person see the future more clearly and plan a more fulfilling retirement for him- or herself. May your own Last Resort be a happy one because you took some of the ideas in this book and made them work for you!

About the Author

Steve Bareham is president of CompComm Inc., a communications firm specializing in publishing and business consulting. He also teaches entrepreneurial skills, human resources and business communication courses to adult learners at Selkirk College.

Prior to launching his own company, Steve worked as an editor and reporter for several Canadian newspapers and in marketing and community relations for TransAlta Power, The B.C. School Trustees Association, and Simon Fraser University.

Steve lives in Nelson, B.C., with his wife, Wendy.

Acknowledgments

Few books are the product of one person's efforts. *The Last Resort* is no exception. Several people were instrumental in providing encouragement to take the idea from fancy to fruition. Still others lent their valuable time and expertise to provide suggestions that have helped ensure accuracy and further clarify financial-planning concepts that can easily become complex and weighty.

These people deserve formal recognition:

First, of course, my wife, Wendy, who, like most writers' wives, was forced to suffer through revision after revision. She cheerfully accepted the book in bits and pieces as it progressed and, somehow, managed to maintain a sense of continuity (and humor) from information given to her at odd hours and in no particular order. She deserves much praise. Her advice and editing aided immeasurably.

Steve Cannon, municipal building inspector and friend, for his critical insights in all areas: finance, life planning, and in particular the chapter dealing with construction details.

Laura Labovitch, CA and B.Comm., investment adviser, Bank of Montreal, and Scott M. Matheson, CA and B.A. Econ., of Money Concepts, Nelson, who checked and double-checked my statistical data and the veracity of the suggested tax-planning strategies.

Rob Thomson, for applying his usual mental acuity in numerous areas.

HarperCollins business editor Don Loney for believing in the merits of *The Last Resort* and for his wisdom and consistently caring attitude through all the stages of publication.

And, finally, Graham MacKinnon, associate executive director of the B.C. School Trustees Association. Graham is a truly gifted strategist and financial planner, who acted unknowingly as mentor to a young, naive colleague who "didn't understand that he didn't understand." Graham could well be the model for Gordon in this book. He deserves credit for helping me, and now, I hope, you as well, to understand that deliberate retirement planning shouldn't be *The Last Resort*.

NOTES

NOTES